YOUR BRAIN IS AMAZING

IS AMAZING

How the Human Mind Works

TRANSLATED BY
LAWRENCE SCHIMEL

ESPERANZA HABINGER

ILLUSTRATED BY **SOLE SEBASTIÁN**

ORCA BOOK PUBLISHERS

CONTENTS

4 INTRODUCTION

A MACROSCOPIC OVERVIEW 6

8 A MICROSCOPIC VIEW

ANALYZING YOUR BRAIN 10

12 I DIDN'T HIT KENTO:
FRONTAL LOBE

I LOVE MY BUNNY VERY MUCH: 14
PARIETAL LOBE

16 I REMEMBER MY GIFTS:
TEMPORAL LOBE

YOUR BRAIN'S EYES: 18
OCCIPITAL LOBE

20 WHAT COORDINATION AND BALANCE!
CEREBELLUM

COULD I FORGET TO BREATHE? 22
BRAIN STEM

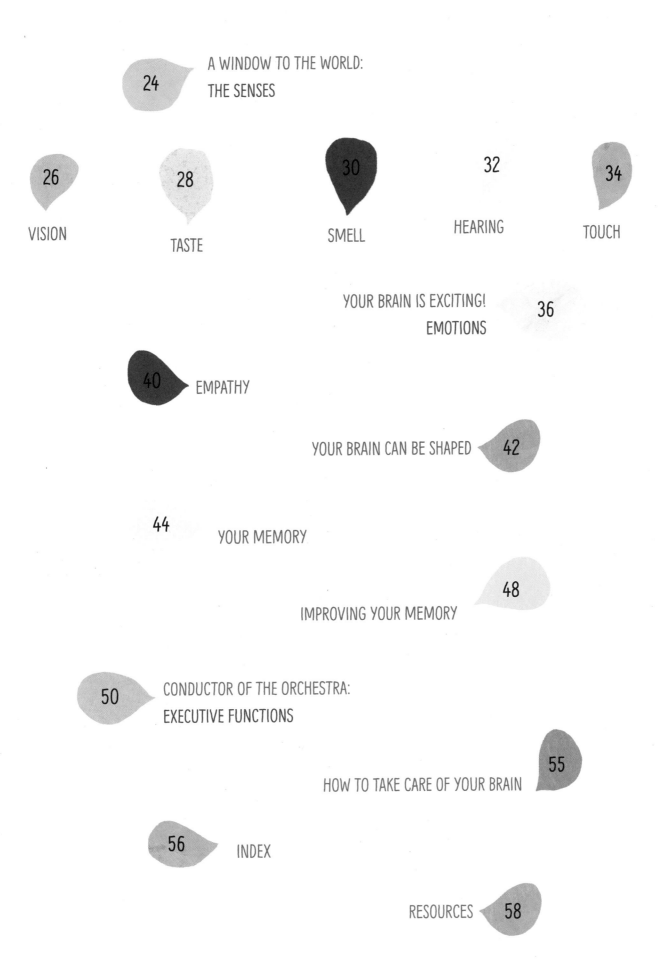

24 A WINDOW TO THE WORLD: THE SENSES

26 VISION

28 TASTE

30 SMELL

32 HEARING

34 TOUCH

YOUR BRAIN IS EXCITING! EMOTIONS 36

40 EMPATHY

YOUR BRAIN CAN BE SHAPED 42

44 YOUR MEMORY

48 IMPROVING YOUR MEMORY

50 CONDUCTOR OF THE ORCHESTRA: EXECUTIVE FUNCTIONS

55 HOW TO TAKE CARE OF YOUR BRAIN

56 INDEX

RESOURCES 58

INTRODUCTION

Stars in the sky, the taste of chocolate, the memories of a holiday, pain after you fall...all these experiences are possible thanks to a part of our bodies that's in our heads—the brain. It's the most complex organ in the whole universe, so studying and understanding it has been (and still is!) very difficult. There are many things we still don't know or understand about it.

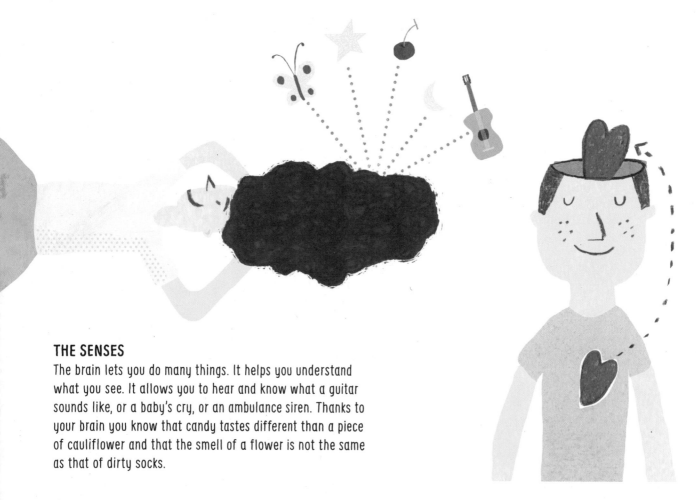

THE SENSES
The brain lets you do many things. It helps you understand what you see. It allows you to hear and know what a guitar sounds like, or a baby's cry, or an ambulance siren. Thanks to your brain you know that candy tastes different than a piece of cauliflower and that the smell of a flower is not the same as that of dirty socks.

IT'S FANTASTIC!
Your brain allows you to have complex language, a sense of humor and even the ability to think about the brain itself. No other living creatures can do all that.

DREAM

BEAT

BREATHE

EMOTIONS
Thanks to your brain you can think, learn and remember. You can also walk, run, dance and move your body any way you want.

It also lets you feel love, sadness, fear and anger. Your emotions are in your brain, and when people say "You have a big heart" to someone who is generous and helps others, what they really mean to say is "You have a big brain!"

4

THOUGHT GENERATOR

The brain has been called a *thought generator*, since it is believed that on average it generates 50,000 thoughts per day—about 2,083 per hour. It can process an image you're looking at in 13 milliseconds, even less time than it takes to blink.

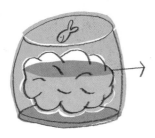

WATER AND FAT

The brain weighs around 3 pounds (1.3 kilograms) and 73 percent of its weight is water. Even with all that water, it's the fattiest organ in the body.

OXYGEN

Your brain needs oxygen all the time. Even five minutes without oxygen causes brain cells to die, causing severe cerebral damage.

ENERGY

The brain represents barely 2 percent of the body's overall weight, but it uses 20 percent of the energy and oxygen your body takes in.

EINSTEIN

Albert Einstein's brain was 10 percent smaller than the average brain, but the density of its neurons was greater than that of most people.

DIFFERENCES

In general, men's brains are 10 percent larger than women's brains. However, the hippocampus, which is the part of the brain related to memory, is typically larger in women.

EVOLUTION

The human brain adapts to its environment. Our earliest human ancestor had a much smaller brain than humans do now—over time it's grown larger. Evolution has not turned us into the strongest or the fastest animal, but it has made us cunning and skilled at surviving on this planet.

THE BIGGEST

In proportion to total body weight, the human brain is the largest of all animal brains. The brain of a sperm whale weighs almost 18 pounds (8 kilograms). If it were 2 percent of the whale's overall body weight, as it is in humans, it would weigh 2,200 pounds (1,000 kilograms)!

A MACROSCOPIC OVERVIEW

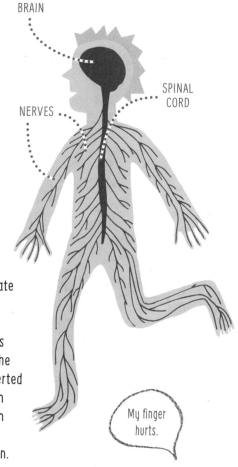

BRAIN

SPINAL CORD

NERVES

CONTROL CENTER

The brain communicates with the rest of your body through a handful of nerves (something like electrical cables). These are located in the spinal cord, which is protected by the spine. Smaller cables branch off from there to help the brain control and direct (like a puppeteer) the rest of your body, muscles, organs, etc.

WHAT LANGUAGE DOES IT USE?

How does one area of the brain communicate with another? What language does it use to control the rest of your body? The only language it knows, understands and uses is electricity. For example, when you listen, the sound waves that enter your ears are converted into electrical signals that travel to the brain through nerves. The same thing happens when you see, smell or taste. All these sensations are turned into electrical impulses that reach your brain.

My finger hurts.

TWO-WAY STREETS

These nerves, or cables, are like two-way streets. The brain sends information—such as when you decide to walk or run, for example— and also receives information.

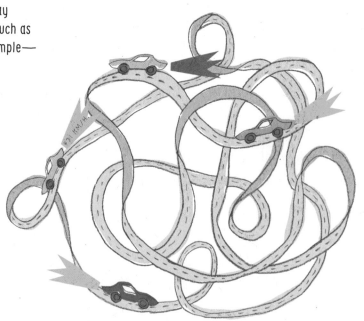

SUPER-FAST

Information from the brain travels at speeds of up to 268 miles per hour (432 kilometers per hour). This is even faster than Formula 1 race cars, which reach a maximum of 240 miles per hour (386 kilometers per hour). Your brain generates around 12 to 25 watts of electricity. This is enough to light up a low-voltage LED light bulb.

WHAT WOULD HAPPEN IF YOU HURT YOUR BRAIN?

If you hurt a finger or a knee, you might feel sad, but you wouldn't stop being you. On the other hand, if a small piece of cerebral tissue in your brain is injured, you could change completely. Depending on the part of the brain hurt, you might no longer recognize your family or know your pet is a dog. You might lose the ability to see or speak, or your personality might be very different than it was before the injury. When the brain changes, you become someone else. You cease to be you. Even if it were possible to do a brain transplant, you would still no longer be you.

WHERE IS IT?

Your brain is in your head, behind your eyes, inside your skull. The skull is a natural helmet that protects your brain from blows and accidents, but it can only protect it to a certain extent. That's why you need to wear a protective helmet when doing certain activities or playing certain sports.

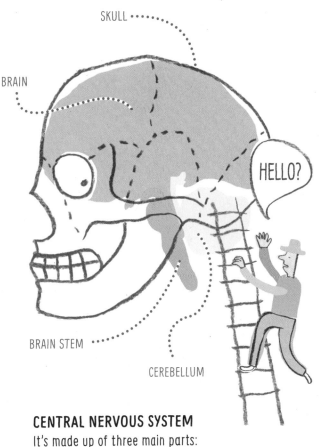

SKULL

BRAIN

HELLO?

BRAIN STEM

CEREBELLUM

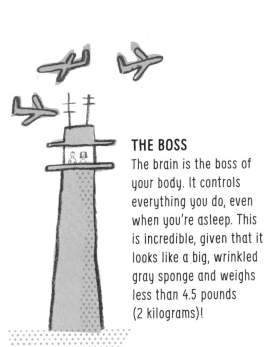

THE BOSS

The brain is the boss of your body. It controls everything you do, even when you're asleep. This is incredible, given that it looks like a big, wrinkled gray sponge and weighs less than 4.5 pounds (2 kilograms)!

CENTRAL NERVOUS SYSTEM

It's made up of three main parts: the brain, the cerebellum and the brain stem.

A MICROSCOPIC VIEW

Just as a wall is made from bricks, the organs of living beings, such as the brain and the heart, are made up of cells. The brain is a big mass of special cells called *neurons*. Some neurons receive messages from the rest of the body—that's why you feel it when something touches you and why you can hear music. Other neurons send messages to the rest of the body—that's why you can walk or run when you decide to, because the brain also controls your movements. The connections between one neuron and another are called *synapses*.

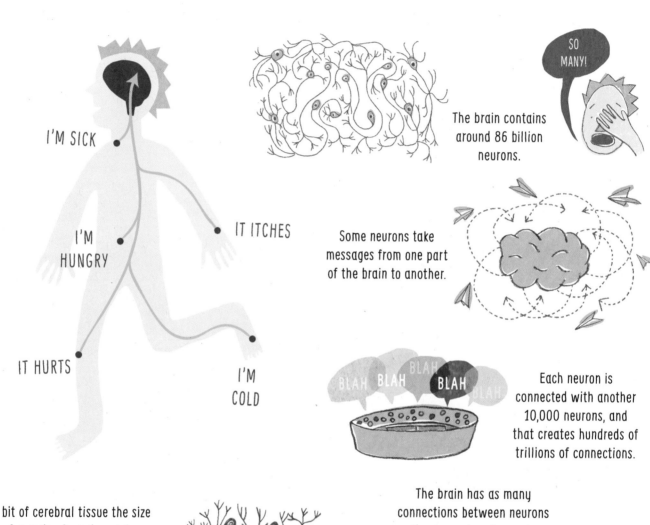

I'M SICK

I'M HUNGRY

IT ITCHES

IT HURTS

I'M COLD

SO MANY!

The brain contains around 86 billion neurons.

Some neurons take messages from one part of the brain to another.

Each neuron is connected with another 10,000 neurons, and that creates hundreds of trillions of connections.

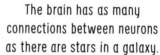

BLAH BLAH BLAH BLAH BLAH

The brain has as many connections between neurons as there are stars in a galaxy.

A bit of cerebral tissue the size of a grain of sand contains 100,000 neurons, with a billion connections between them.

There are thousands of us.

And we're connected.

There are various types of cells in the brain, not just neurons. There is another kind called *glia cells*.

GROWTH OF THE BRAIN

During pregnancy, 250,000 new neurons are created per minute in a baby's brain. Babies are born with the same number of neurons an adult has. The difference is that only a small number of those neurons are connected.

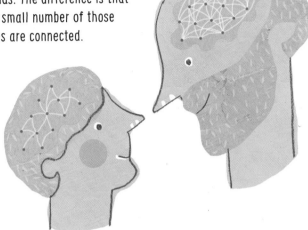

80%   100%

BABY HEADS

Babies have large heads compared to their body size, and this enables them to sustain the brain's rapid growth. A two-year-old's brain is 80 percent the size of an adult brain.

TAKE ADVANTAGE!

At three years old, a child's brain has 1,000 trillion connections, which is about twice as many as adults have. Between the ages of three and ten, brain activity is very intense, and although new connections are formed throughout your entire life, the brain can never learn and manage new skills or adapt to setbacks as easily as it does at this time.

Happy Cerebral Maturity

25

CEREBRAL MATURITY

Teenagers' brains are not fully developed. The front third of the brain (where the frontal lobes are) is still taking shape. At approximately 25 years old, the brain becomes fully mature. After 25, it starts to slowly decline.

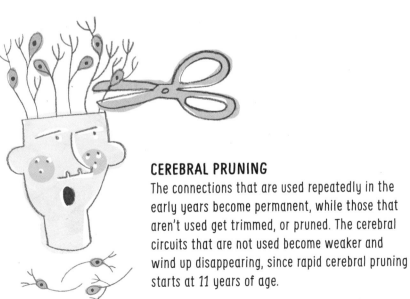

CEREBRAL PRUNING

The connections that are used repeatedly in the early years become permanent, while those that aren't used get trimmed, or pruned. The cerebral circuits that are not used become weaker and wind up disappearing, since rapid cerebral pruning starts at 11 years of age.

ANALYZING YOUR BRAIN

The brain can be divided in ways that help us study and understand it. It can be split into halves, the front brain and the back brain, or into the right hemisphere and the left hemisphere. Within these hemispheres are four sectors, called the *cerebral lobes*. The individual lobes and hemispheres serve different purposes. Each has a unique function, and although we'll talk about them separately, they always work together.

BACK

FRONT

FRONT BRAIN AND BACK BRAIN

The back half of the brain has various "windows" to recognize and interpret what is going on outside. With this half of your brain you look, listen and touch. The front half of your brain receives the information from the back brain, and based on that information, you think and make decisions.

R | L

BRAIN HALVES: LEFT AND RIGHT HEMISPHERE

Dividing the brain down the middle into halves, you have the right hemisphere, which controls the left side of your body, and the left hemisphere, which controls the right side of your body. This means that if you move your right arm, it is the left hemisphere controlling the movement. Both halves communicate and exchange information with each other.

RIGHT HEMISPHERE

This is where you find people's creativity, passions and dreams. It is called the *intuitive* or the *free-spirit hemisphere*.

LEFT HEMISPHERE

This is the part of the brain that guides rational thought, precision and order. It is called the *logical* or *scientific hemisphere*.

THE FOUR ROOMS: CEREBRAL LOBES

Every cerebral hemisphere has four sectors, called *lobes*. Although the lobes work together, they are each in charge of different tasks. Together, all the areas of the brain allow you to think analytically, see the consequences of your actions, plan for the future and enjoy life. In short, they make you human.

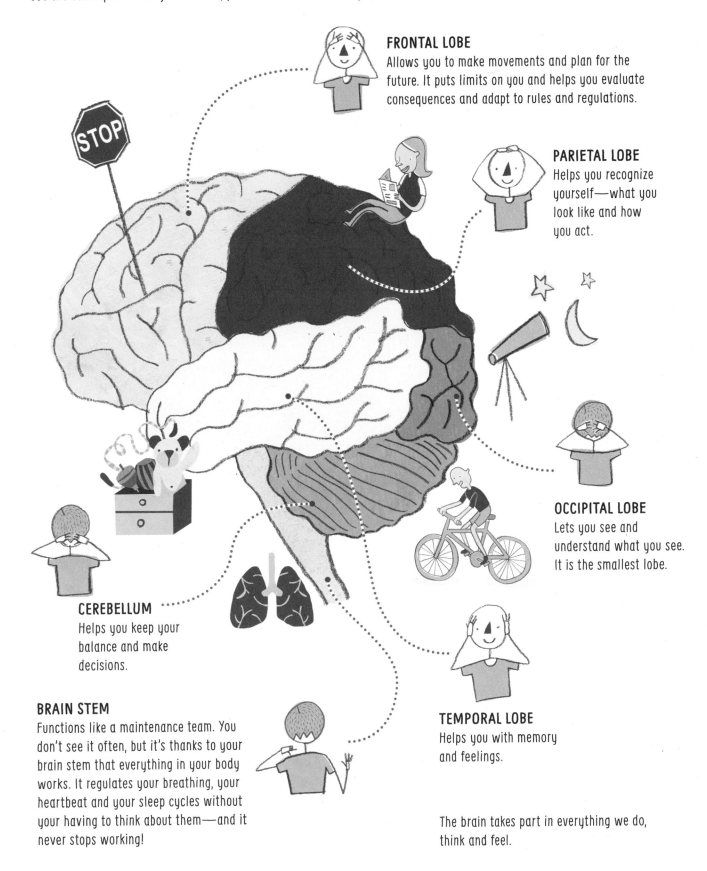

FRONTAL LOBE
Allows you to make movements and plan for the future. It puts limits on you and helps you evaluate consequences and adapt to rules and regulations.

PARIETAL LOBE
Helps you recognize yourself—what you look like and how you act.

OCCIPITAL LOBE
Lets you see and understand what you see. It is the smallest lobe.

CEREBELLUM
Helps you keep your balance and make decisions.

TEMPORAL LOBE
Helps you with memory and feelings.

BRAIN STEM
Functions like a maintenance team. You don't see it often, but it's thanks to your brain stem that everything in your body works. It regulates your breathing, your heartbeat and your sleep cycles without your having to think about them—and it never stops working!

The brain takes part in everything we do, think and feel.

I DIDN'T HIT KENTO
FRONTAL LOBE

Kento sits behind me in class. While the teacher explains a concept at the board, he pulls my hair, throws things at me, puts his shoes on my chair and wiggles his legs constantly. He just won't leave me alone! I don't want to say anything in case I get called a tattletale. But the other day he snuck up on me and pushed me so hard that if I hadn't grabbed on to a nearby tree, I'd have fallen down. I was so angry! I counted to 10, remembering how I would get in trouble if I hit him back. So instead I decided to ask for help from the yard duty. She congratulated me, because instead of hitting Kento and dumping my anger on him, I'd turned to an adult. That is thanks to my frontal lobe.

SOME FUNCTIONS OF THE FRONTAL LOBE

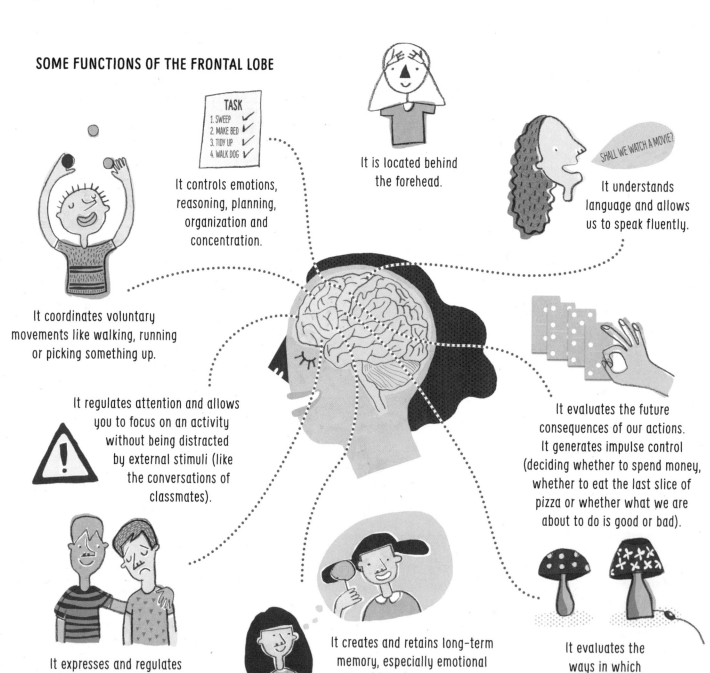

It coordinates voluntary movements like walking, running or picking something up.

It controls emotions, reasoning, planning, organization and concentration.

It is located behind the forehead.

SHALL WE WATCH A MOVIE?

It understands language and allows us to speak fluently.

It regulates attention and allows you to focus on an activity without being distracted by external stimuli (like the conversations of classmates).

It evaluates the future consequences of our actions. It generates impulse control (deciding whether to spend money, whether to eat the last slice of pizza or whether what we are about to do is good or bad).

It expresses and regulates emotions, in addition to understanding other people's emotions (empathy).

It creates and retains long-term memory, especially emotional memory (like how you felt at a specific moment).

It evaluates the ways in which different objects are alike and different.

12

USE YOUR FRONTAL LOBE

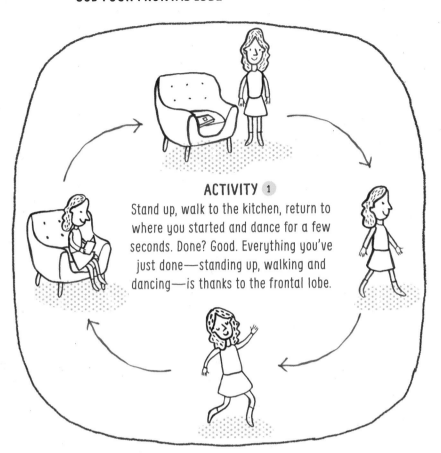

ACTIVITY 1

Stand up, walk to the kitchen, return to where you started and dance for a few seconds. Done? Good. Everything you've just done—standing up, walking and dancing—is thanks to the frontal lobe.

ACTIVITY 2

Imagine you're shopping at the supermarket and you run into someone you have a crush on (but have never spoken to). Your heart starts racing, and you feel butterflies in your stomach. Do you imagine yourself running through the aisles, shouting that you're in love? Do you imagine yourself approaching that person, singing a love song and then saying you love them? Do you think it would be terrible to lose your self-control that way? You don't lose it, thanks to your frontal lobe.

PHINEAS GAGE

Damage to the frontal lobe can produce immediate changes in personality. In 1848 a worker named Phineas Gage suffered a serious accident—an iron rod pierced his head and destroyed much of his frontal lobe. Miraculously he recovered from the accident, but his personality was permanently changed. He stopped being a nice person and a good worker. He was lazy and rude until he died. The ways a person may behave differently than they used to depends on the sector of the frontal lobe that is damaged.

THANKS, FRONTAL LOBE!

Thanks to your frontal lobe, you have the ability to control your behavior and your emotions. It's also responsible for your voluntary movements and your ability to resolve problems. This lobe has a lot to do with what makes us human, because it takes part in everything from our movements to our intelligence. It helps us anticipate the consequences of our actions and plan future actions.

I LOVE MY BUNNY VERY MUCH
PARIETAL LOBE

My bunny, Lola, has the softest fur, and it's very nice to pet her. Sometimes I imagine that I'm touching a cloud. It feels like cotton, but Lola's hair is long and thick, so I can tell the difference between fur and cotton. And she is so warm—I wish my sheets were like her. But they're not, and in winter they are cold and somewhat stiff. But Lola loves to sleep snuggled at my neck, so her fluffy warmth is always with me. Thanks to my parietal lobe, I can feel how marvelous Lola is and tell the difference between her and cotton.

SOME FUNCTIONS OF THE PARIETAL LOBE

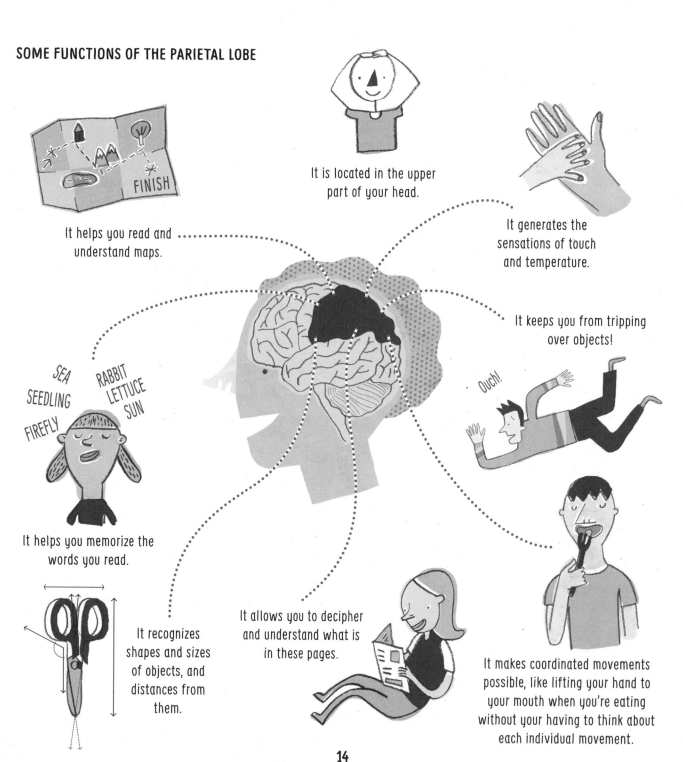

It helps you read and understand maps.

It is located in the upper part of your head.

It generates the sensations of touch and temperature.

It keeps you from tripping over objects!

Ouch!

It helps you memorize the words you read.

SEA SEEDLING FIREFLY RABBIT LETTUCE SUN

It recognizes shapes and sizes of objects, and distances from them.

It allows you to decipher and understand what is in these pages.

It makes coordinated movements possible, like lifting your hand to your mouth when you're eating without your having to think about each individual movement.

USE YOUR PARIETAL LOBE

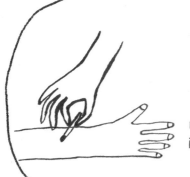

ACTIVITY 1
Find any object (a pencil, a bit of cotton, a toothbrush, etc.) and ask a friend or family member to touch you with it somewhere on your arm while you have your eyes closed. Did you feel it? Did you know what part of your arm was in contact with the object?

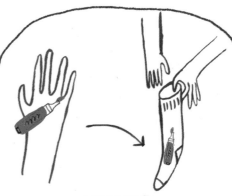

ACTIVITY 3
Ask a friend or family member to hide an object inside a sock without telling you what it is. Put your hand in the sock and try to figure out what the object is without looking. Were you able to?

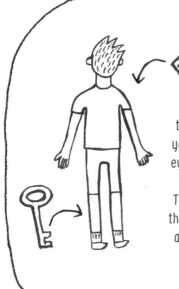

ACTIVITY 2
Ask a friend or family member to pick two items that are the same (two matchsticks, two coins, two keys, etc.) and touch you with them in two different places on your body at the same time while you have your eyes closed. Could you feel two points of contact and the areas where the objects touched you? There are areas of your body where you can feel the two contacts even if they are very close (such as the tips of your fingers) and others, like your back, where despite there being two points of contact, you only feel one.

RIGHT OR LEFT?
The effects of damage to the parietal lobe will vary depending on whether the damage is to one or both lobes and if it is to the lobe in the right or left hemisphere. For example, if a person hurts their right lobe, they will have difficulty protecting their body because they will no longer feel their left side. If they touch something very hot, they won't realize it, and this could result in a serious burn—which they won't feel either.

THANKS, PARIETAL LOBE!
The parietal lobe interprets the information it receives and lets you recognize objects you touch or that touch you. It also takes part in your ability to read and write and recognize the different parts of the body. Thanks to your parietal lobe, you can distinguish between two different things without needing to look at them.

I REMEMBER MY GIFTS
TEMPORAL LOBE

Joey is my dog, and when he arrived he was little and playful. He loved to chew my slippers and was an expert at finding them. He also went to the bathroom everywhere and even wet my bed one day. But now Joey is much bigger and doesn't eat my shoes and doesn't pee inside the house. The ability to remember Joey when he was a puppy, is because of my temporal lobe.

SOME FUNCTIONS OF THE TEMPORAL LOBE

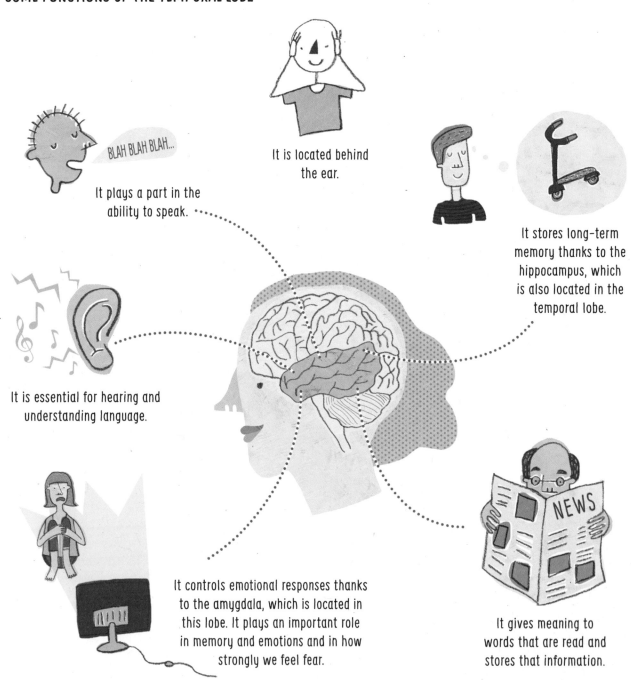

It plays a part in the ability to speak.

It is located behind the ear.

It stores long-term memory thanks to the hippocampus, which is also located in the temporal lobe.

It is essential for hearing and understanding language.

It controls emotional responses thanks to the amygdala, which is located in this lobe. It plays an important role in memory and emotions and in how strongly we feel fear.

It gives meaning to words that are read and stores that information.

USE YOUR TEMPORAL LOBE

ACTIVITY 1

Ask a friend or family member what they're doing or to tell you the best thing that has happened to them over the past few days. You can ask them whatever you want. Did you listen to and understand their answer?

ACTIVITY 2

Ask a friend or family member to make different sounds (clapping, whistling, snapping their fingers, barking, etc.) and, with your eyes closed, try to recognize those sounds. This will likely be easy for you. That is thanks to the temporal lobe.

I CAN HARDLY UNDERSTAND ANYTHING

The effects of damage to the temporal lobe depend on which sector is affected. Damage can cause memory problems, changes in personality, difficulties in understanding what is read, an inability to speak and to understand spoken language, and a lack of facial recognition, among other things.

THANKS, TEMPORAL LOBE!

One of the functions of the temporal lobe is giving you the ability to hear and also understand what you hear. Thanks to the temporal lobe, you can listen to and enjoy music. It is responsible for your ability to recognize different sounds and memorize them.

17

YOUR BRAIN'S EYES
OCCIPITAL LOBE

I really like to visit my grandparents. Their house is nice, and they always make me yummy things to eat. Sometimes, as I eat a cookie, I look at my grandfather. He is tall and wide and has white hair. He is sitting down, reading a very thick book, a couple of feet away from me. When he hears my voice or my grandmother going out into the garden, he immediately stops reading and looks at me or out the window to find my grandmother. Then he resumes reading as if nothing happened. I can tell you this about my grandfather thanks to my occipital lobe.

Look at everything around you. The ability to see your surroundings is because of the occipital lobe.

SOME FUNCTIONS OF THE OCCIPITAL LOBE

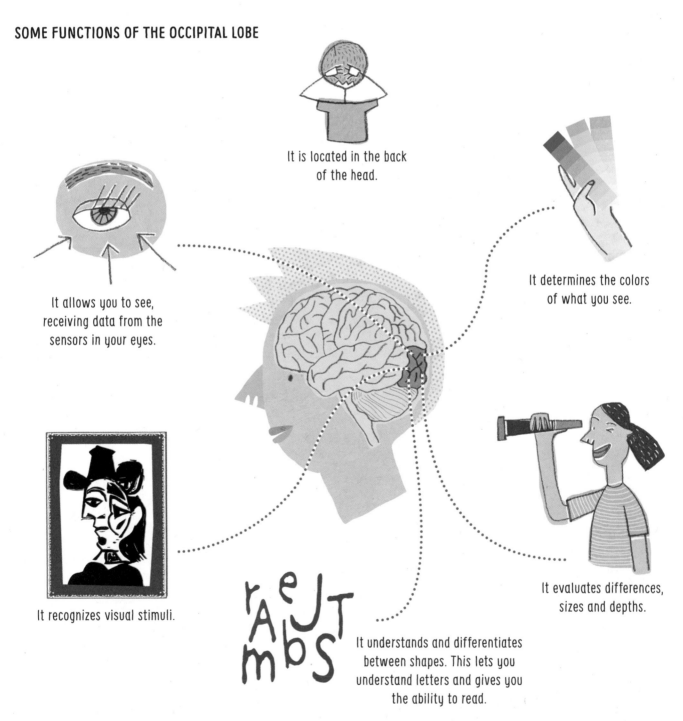

It is located in the back of the head.

It allows you to see, receiving data from the sensors in your eyes.

It determines the colors of what you see.

It recognizes visual stimuli.

It evaluates differences, sizes and depths.

It understands and differentiates between shapes. This lets you understand letters and gives you the ability to read.

USE YOUR OCCIPITAL LOBE

ACTIVITY 1

Make note of how long it takes you to travel a certain distance—from your bedroom to the bathroom, for example. Then put on a blindfold and, with the help of a walking stick, travel the same path. How long did it take you with your eyes closed? Probably much longer, because you had to move slowly and carefully so you wouldn't bump into anything.

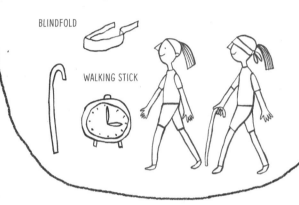

BLINDFOLD

WALKING STICK

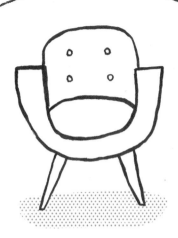

ACTIVITY 2

Look at a piece of furniture nearby. You recognize it, since you know its size, shape and color. Pick up a book with photos or illustrations of objects and look at those objects. You also recognize them, or, if one is very strange, you can imagine what it is and what it might be for. Look for some object or an image of an unknown object and ask your friends what they think it is. Probably a few of them will have similar ideas.

MY EYES ARE FINE, BUT I CAN'T SEE

The effects of damage to the occipital lobe vary based on the sector affected. It might cause complete or partial blindness and the inability to recognize what you see. It might produce visual hallucinations (seeing things that are not really there) or visual illusions (seeing something different from what is really there), or it might change how you perceive the size of objects you see or make you see them without color or with abnormal coloration.

THANKS, OCCIPITAL LOBE!

The occipital lobe is very powerful—it lets you recognize the world around you and enjoy it (if it's something pleasant) or protect yourself (if it's something dangerous). It lets you understand and distinguish what you see, recognize colors and shapes and then give them meaning.

WHAT COORDINATION AND BALANCE!
CEREBELLUM

Every weekend I go to the park to play. I love being outside! And also there are other boys and girls there to play games with—like soccer or volleyball. A little while ago, in that same park, my mother showed me how to rollerblade. Do you know why I can do all these things, like running, kicking the ball or rollerblading? Is it because I have the best in-line skates in the world? No! I can do these and many other activities that need coordination and balance because I have a cerebellum.

SOME FUNCTIONS OF THE CEREBELLUM

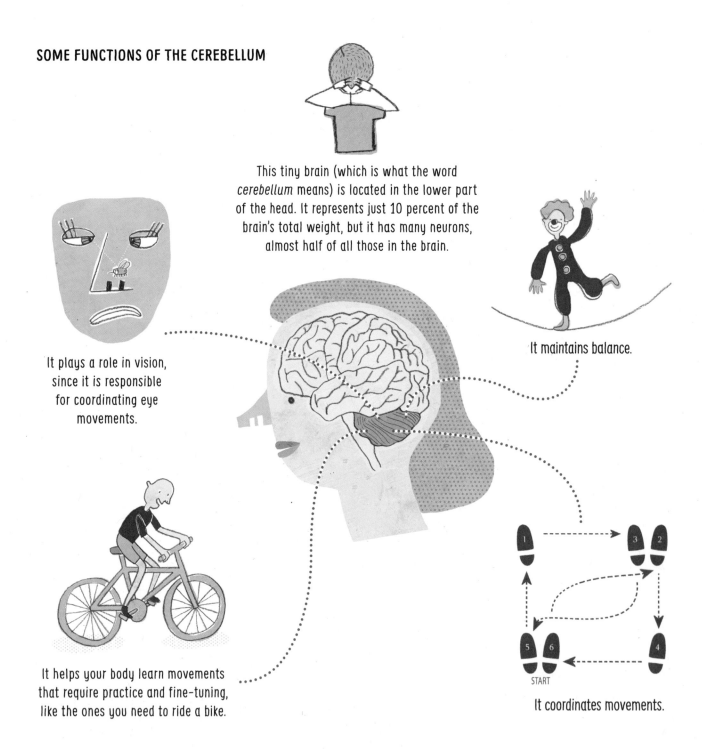

This tiny brain (which is what the word *cerebellum* means) is located in the lower part of the head. It represents just 10 percent of the brain's total weight, but it has many neurons, almost half of all those in the brain.

It plays a role in vision, since it is responsible for coordinating eye movements.

It maintains balance.

It helps your body learn movements that require practice and fine-tuning, like the ones you need to ride a bike.

It coordinates movements.

START

20

USE YOUR CEREBELLUM

ACTIVITY 1

Take the keys to a door and put them in your pocket. Then find the middle of that room and spin around in place a few times. When you stop, you'll likely feel a bit dizzy. Walk carefully toward the door and try to put the key in the lock. Since you're dizzy, your gait will be a little unstable—you'll walk with your legs spread apart, swaying your body to feel more secure. It will be difficult to stick the key in the lock. This feeling of instability is what you would feel all the time if your cerebellum was damaged.

ACTIVITY 2

Find a small cup and fill it with clips of different colors, coins of different denominations and buttons of different shapes. Then, with one hand and a tweezer, without the help of your other hand, separate the items from the original cup and put them in other cups or piles—for example, one cup with red clips, one with green, one cup with dimes, another with nickels, etc. The activity is completed when all the objects are separated according to their characteristics and the original cup is empty. You'll have realized that you need to make precise and coordinated movements to do this activity. You can do that thanks to the cerebellum.

CLUMSY OR INJURED?

You can tell when someone has damaged their cerebellum because they will lack muscle control and coordination. They'll also have difficulty walking and talking.

THANKS, CEREBELLUM!

Thanks to your cerebellum, you can run and dance, and if you practice enough, you can skateboard, ski, rollerblade, play the piano or guitar—in short, all the activities that require a lot of coordination and fine movement are possible thanks to your cerebellum.

COULD I FORGET TO BREATHE?
BRAIN STEM

Don't worry. That won't happen, because you have a brain stem. How do we breathe and keep our hearts beating even though we don't think about it? Because, fortunately, we have a brain stem that takes care of all the functions necessary to maintain life—breathing, digesting food, sending blood throughout the body (pumped by the heart), sleeping, swallowing and controlling blood pressure. The brain stem connects the brain with the spinal cord. Motor neurons (which transmit information from the brain to extremities) and sensory neutrons (which carry messages from the senses to the brain) travel via the brain stem.

SOME FUNCTIONS OF THE BRAIN STEM

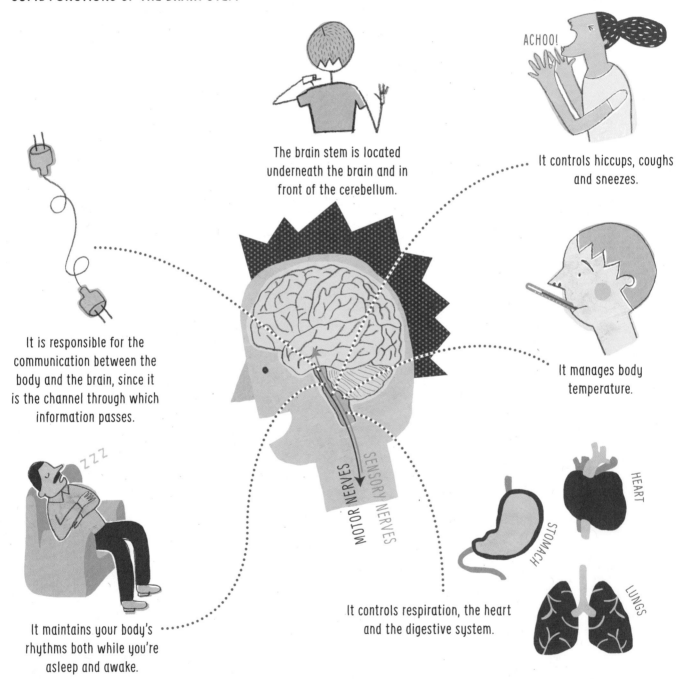

The brain stem is located underneath the brain and in front of the cerebellum.

It controls hiccups, coughs and sneezes.

It is responsible for the communication between the body and the brain, since it is the channel through which information passes.

It manages body temperature.

MOTOR NERVES

SENSORY NERVES

STOMACH

HEART

LUNGS

It maintains your body's rhythms both while you're asleep and awake.

It controls respiration, the heart and the digestive system.

22

ACTIVITY 1

Sit calmly and place the tips of the fingers of your right hand on the underside of your left wrist. You'll feel your pulse (the beats of your heart). Count how many times your heart beats in one minute. Is it 70 times? 80?

Now jump up and down 15 times and then take your pulse again. Did you see how it went up? Do you see how the heart adapts how hard it works according to your body's needs or activities?

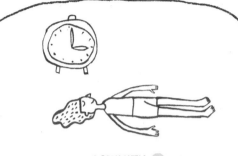

ACTIVITY 2

Sit or lie down calmly and pay attention to how many times you breathe in one minute. Notice that you are not thinking about the fact that you need to breathe in order to live, yet you do breathe. This happens all the time, even when you're asleep.

INVOLUNTARY WORK

The heart beats automatically—it doesn't need you to be thinking about it all the time in order to beat. If you pay attention, you'll notice that your pulse is faster after doing exercise (riding a bike, running, playing ball). This is because your heart has to send more blood through your body.

Damage to the brain stem can produce problems in the heart's rhythm and difficulty in breathing and swallowing. It can also cause paralysis in your limbs! That's because the motor neurons, which control your movements, pass through the brain stem.

The brain stem is in charge of the basic functions crucial to your survival.

THANKS, BRAIN STEM!

It is in charge of all the functions you need to stay alive. It allows your heart to beat, your lungs to breathe and your stomach to digest food. And, best of all, you don't have to think about these things—they happen automatically! All the information between the brain and the rest of the body circulates through the brain stem.

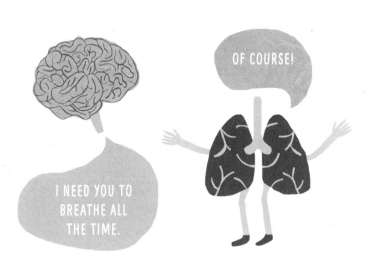

OF COURSE!

I NEED YOU TO BREATHE ALL THE TIME.

A WINDOW TO THE WORLD
THE SENSES

Your tongue, your skin, your nose, your eyes and your ears are external sensory organs. They get information from the outside world and transmit it to you, allowing you to be aware of yourself and what surrounds you.

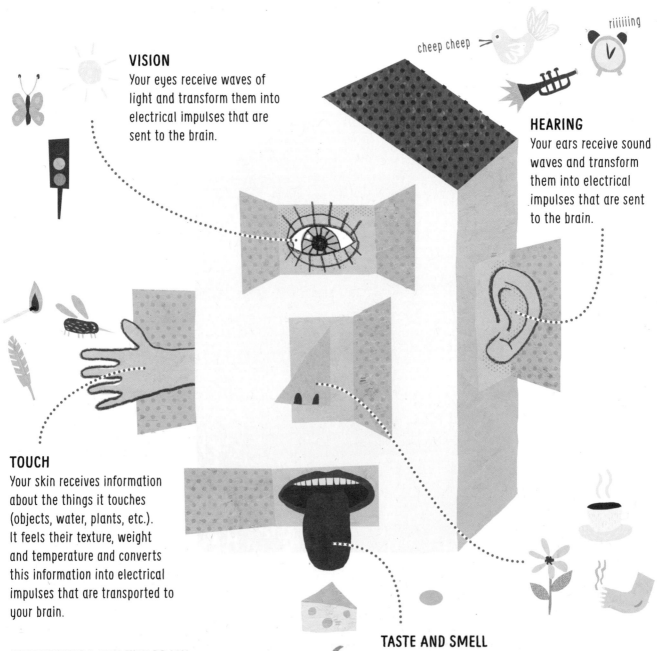

cheep cheep

riiiiiing

VISION
Your eyes receive waves of light and transform them into electrical impulses that are sent to the brain.

HEARING
Your ears receive sound waves and transform them into electrical impulses that are sent to the brain.

TOUCH
Your skin receives information about the things it touches (objects, water, plants, etc.). It feels their texture, weight and temperature and converts this information into electrical impulses that are transported to your brain.

EVERYTHING WITH THE BRAIN
Notice how your ears, eyes, skin, nose and tongue all work as translators. They convert stimuli (sound waves, light waves, the characteristics of objects, molecules that you smell or taste) into electrical impulses that are assigned meaning when they reach your brain. You then understand what you hear, see, feel, smell or taste.

TASTE AND SMELL
The molecules of food that reach your tongue are registered by taste buds. The molecules given off by the scents of objects are registered by receptors in your nose. All this information is converted into electrical impulses that are sent to your brain.

WANT TO EXPERIMENT AND DISCOVER THE IMPORTANCE OF THE SENSORY ORGANS?
This is a simple but powerful exercise.

Look for someplace very quiet in your house and stand there for a few minutes. Put on a blindfold and place earplugs in your ears. Keep your mouth closed and breathe gently through your nose. The only things that connect you with the world around you are the contact of your feet with the floor and the feel of the blindfold, earplugs and clothes on your body.

If we could eliminate the sense of touch (which is active in this experience, because you feel the earplugs, the blindfold, your clothes, the contact with the floor), you wouldn't feel anything but the air entering through your nose.

But discounting what you feel through touch, which we can't eliminate, you are isolated from the world—you don't see anything, you don't hear sounds, you don't smell and you don't know the textures of things. In other words, you know almost nothing about the world around you.

VERY IMPORTANT
That's what the senses are for—to help us know and understand the world around us and let us move through it independently and safely. We can recognize places, situations, changes, dangers or pleasant things and react to them. Sometimes the reactions are so fast they seem automatic, like when something burns you and you pull your hand back. Or when you smell a flower and feel pleasure even before you've consciously registered that you're smelling a flower.

VISION

I like to dress well and choose clothing colors that go together. Sometimes I paint my nails the same color. My sister laughs at me, but she matches her soccer shirts to her pants.

Thanks to the eyes, you can distinguish the colors, shapes and sizes of everything you observe around you. The brain is what processes what you see. The function of the eye is to translate the vibrations of light into electrical impulses that are transmitted to the brain.

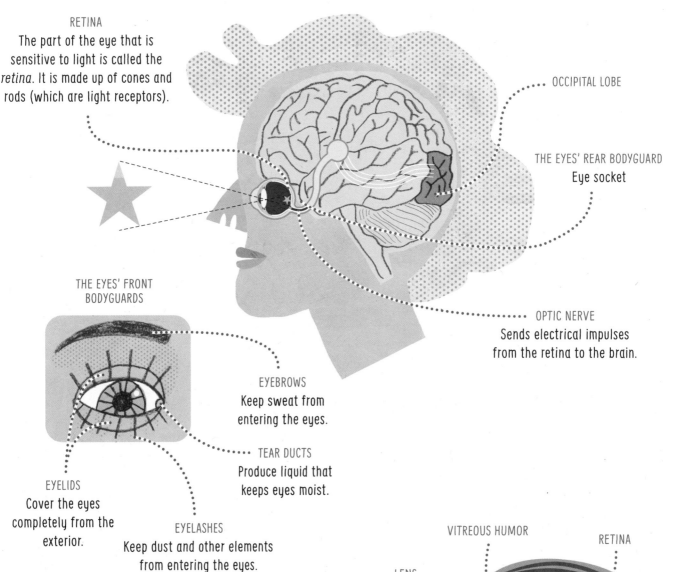

RETINA
The part of the eye that is sensitive to light is called the *retina*. It is made up of cones and rods (which are light receptors).

OCCIPITAL LOBE

THE EYES' REAR BODYGUARD
Eye socket

OPTIC NERVE
Sends electrical impulses from the retina to the brain.

THE EYES' FRONT BODYGUARDS

EYEBROWS
Keep sweat from entering the eyes.

TEAR DUCTS
Produce liquid that keeps eyes moist.

EYELIDS
Cover the eyes completely from the exterior.

EYELASHES
Keep dust and other elements from entering the eyes.

THE EYE IS A TRANSLATOR

Light rays enter your eyes through a transparent layer that protects them, called the *cornea*. From there the rays pass through a natural window (your pupil) until they reach the lens. Then they pass through the vitreous humor (a transparent gel) to reach the retina, which has photoreceptors (cones and rods) that receive the light. The retina is where light waves are processed to transmit them to the brain via the optic nerve.

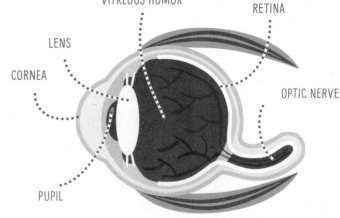

VITREOUS HUMOR

RETINA

LENS

CORNEA

OPTIC NERVE

PUPIL

TWO EYES ARE BETTER THAN ONE

Two eyes help you perceive depth and determine which objects are closer or farther away than others. It is easier to use both eyes, since each eye looks at the image from a different angle.

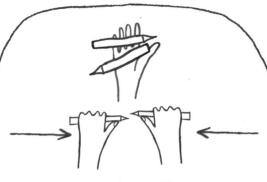

ACTIVITY 1

Hold a pencil in each hand and stretch both arms forward. Keep the pencils 8 to 12 inches (20 to 30 centimeters) apart. Close one eye and try to touch the tip of one pencil with the tip of the other. Repeat the same thing with both eyes open. Is it easier with both eyes open or with only one? You can try this experiment with your fingers instead of pencils.

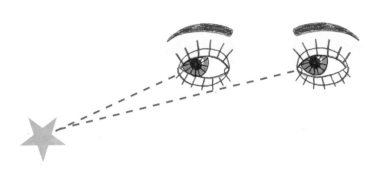

TWO SPHERES

The eyes are two spheres protected by the eye sockets of the cranium (skull). Their round shape helps them work together, which wouldn't happen if they were irregularly shaped (pyramids or cubes).

OPTICAL ILLUSIONS

Sometimes what we see is not what is really in front of us. Illusions are images with colors, light or patterns that are misinterpreted by our brains, creating an image that does not match the true image.

Look at the image at the right. Which yellow line is longer? If you measure them with a ruler, you'll find they're the same length. This optical illusion is produced because the red lines become smaller to suggest moving into the distance. From this perspective, it would seem that the upper yellow line is longer than the bottom one, but they're the same size!

Look at this image. How many triangles can you see? There are none! There are only angles.

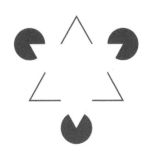

TRICKY

Looking at these images, you can discover how the brain interprets information incorrectly.

TASTE

On the last Friday of every month, we have a special meal in my house. Sometimes it's lasagna, other times roast chicken and sometimes even fried fish! I love these three dishes. However, on other days I'm fed different foods—sometimes mashed potatoes and sausage, or beans. Once it was broccoli pie! I don't like the taste of broccoli, but my best friend, Amara, loves it.

Humans can distinguish different tastes thanks to our tongues.

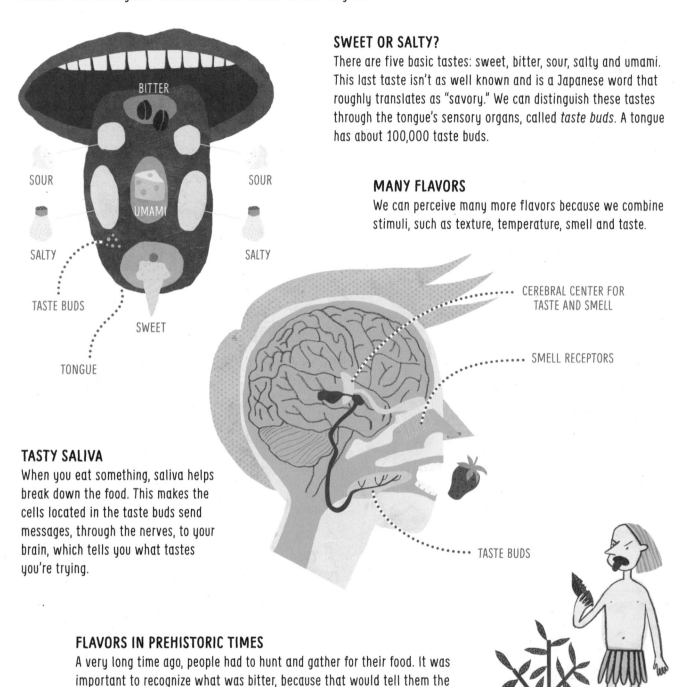

BITTER

SOUR

SOUR

UMAMI

SALTY

SALTY

TASTE BUDS

SWEET

TONGUE

SWEET OR SALTY?
There are five basic tastes: sweet, bitter, sour, salty and umami. This last taste isn't as well known and is a Japanese word that roughly translates as "savory." We can distinguish these tastes through the tongue's sensory organs, called *taste buds*. A tongue has about 100,000 taste buds.

MANY FLAVORS
We can perceive many more flavors because we combine stimuli, such as texture, temperature, smell and taste.

CEREBRAL CENTER FOR TASTE AND SMELL

SMELL RECEPTORS

TASTE BUDS

TASTY SALIVA
When you eat something, saliva helps break down the food. This makes the cells located in the taste buds send messages, through the nerves, to your brain, which tells you what tastes you're trying.

FLAVORS IN PREHISTORIC TIMES
A very long time ago, people had to hunt and gather for their food. It was important to recognize what was bitter, because that would tell them the unknown food was toxic. Recognizing something sweet allowed them to choose foods that gave them quick calories, which helped them run away from dangerous animals.

PARTNERS

The sense of taste is closely tied to the sense of smell. The next time you're eating, cover your nose and see if you can figure out the flavors of the food. Probably not, because taste is a combination of your senses of taste and smell.

IMPOSSIBLE TASTE

Did you know that what we see influences our perception of the flavor of things? An experiment proved this. Three glasses were filled, one with a yellow drink, one with a red drink and the last with a transparent drink. A fourth glass had fizzy water with orange dye added to it, so it looked like orange soda. The people who tried the different drinks all claimed that the glass with fizzy water tasted of orange! Impossible! But this shows how vision influences the sense of taste.

ACTIVITY 1

Dry your tongue with a paper towel, place a bit of food on it (salt, sugar, bits of cookie, some drops of lemon juice, etc.) and try to detect the flavor. Try different kinds of food. Between each different flavor, rinse your mouth with water and dry it again. You probably won't taste the flavors, since in order for food to have taste, its components need to dissolve and mix with liquid (saliva).

This happens because your saliva breaks up the flavors and sends the information to the brain. Without saliva, that doesn't happen.

PAPER   SALT   SUGAR   COOKIES   WATER

ACTIVITY 2

Dip a cotton swab in salt water and lightly touch different places on a friend's tongue until you find the spot where they most clearly notice the taste. Repeat the experiment with other solutions, such as sugar water, vinegar or lemon juice, or tonic water, using a new cotton swab and having them wash out their mouth with plain water between each test. Do the same tests on your own tongue.

Are there sections of the tongue that are more sensitive to specific flavors? Are all the sections equally sensitive to different flavors? If you found differences, draw the sensitive areas for your own tongue and your friend's.

Are they the same? Different regions of the tongue are more sensitive to different kinds of flavors.

PLAIN WATER AND SALT OR SUGAR WATER   VINEGAR OR LEMON   TONIC WATER

COTTON SWABS   PAPER   PENCIL

SMELL

Walking home today I noticed a delicious smell—baked apple pie! So yummy! I wanted to eat it right away. But then an unpleasant smell suddenly hit me—in front of me, a dog pooping. I lost my appetite completely!

Your sense of smell is in charge of perceiving and recognizing scents. It is the most sensitive of all the senses. The molecules of scent are called *odorants*, and only a few are needed to stimulate an olfactory cell. Smelling the scent of a rose, perfume or freshly baked bread (so yummy!) is possible thanks to your nose and your brain.

HOW DO WE SMELL?
Scent molecules are in the air, and they enter your nose via your nasal passages when you breathe. Once there they come into contact with the olfactory receptors and are transformed into electrical impulses that reach the brain via the olfactory nerve. It is your brain that recognizes what you are smelling.

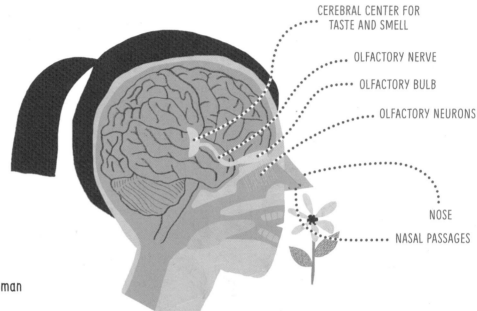

CEREBRAL CENTER FOR TASTE AND SMELL

OLFACTORY NERVE

OLFACTORY BULB

OLFACTORY NEURONS

NOSE

NASAL PASSAGES

SMELL IS IMPORTANT
The sense of smell is important for human survival. Thanks to it we can detect unpleasant smells usually associated with toxic substances, polluting gases, decaying food, smoke or mold—all things that aren't good for us. The sense of smell also reinforces memory, since scents leave memories.

UP TO 10,000 SCENTS
Humans can detect up to 10,000 different scents, but not all people are alike, and there are some who find it much more difficult to recognize scents.

DID YOU KNOW...

...that millions of people in the world lack the ability to smell? This is called *anosmia*.

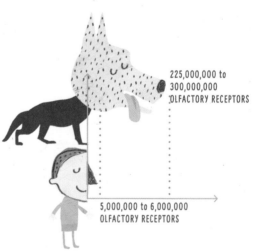

225,000,000 to 300,000,000 OLFACTORY RECEPTORS

5,000,000 to 6,000,000 OLFACTORY RECEPTORS

...that humans have around 5 to 6 million olfactory receptors? A German shepherd has around 225 to 300 million!

ACTIVITY ①

Find 10 things with a scent, some edible and others that are not—for example, orange peel, banana, chocolate, coffee, vanilla, garlic, onion, cinnamon, ginger, perfume and mint leaves. Put them in separate small containers that are not transparent, such as yogurt containers. Put one of the items into two containers. Cover them with tin foil and poke tiny holes so the smell can come out. Ask your friends if they can recognize what is in each container and to pick which two smell alike. We detect and differentiate multiple distinct scents thanks to our sense of smell, which is very sensitive.

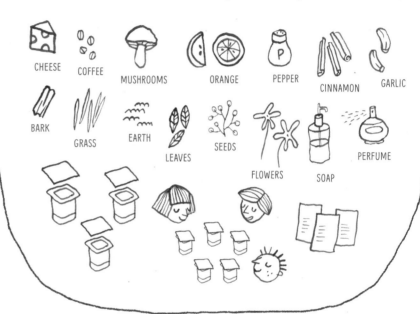

CHEESE · COFFEE · MUSHROOMS · ORANGE · PEPPER · CINNAMON · GARLIC · BARK · GRASS · EARTH · LEAVES · SEEDS · FLOWERS · SOAP · PERFUME

HOW USEFUL IS MY SENSE OF SMELL?

Your nose and your brain help one another in order to help you choose good things to eat. Today it's easy to eat well because we buy the majority of our food in stores. But it wasn't always like this. Imagine prehistoric peoples searching for food!

ACTIVITY ②

Take three freshly washed white T-shirts and mark the back of each label with the first initial of three friends. Ask each of those friends to wear their assigned T-shirt for a few hours, taking care not to get them dirty. Then ask them to give you the T-shirts they've worn. Mix up the shirts.

OMAR · EMILY · JAMES

O · E · J

Now each of your friends, using only their sense of smell, must try to identify the T-shirt they wore. Although this might seem like a strange experiment, you'll be surprised by the results. They'll likely be able to do this, because each person has an individual smell. It's like a fingerprint. We could say we each have a "scent print."

HEARING

My mother likes to listen to classical music, especially piano pieces. My brother likes to play guitar and sing pop songs. I enjoy listening to both. But what I like most of all is to listen to the purring of my cat.

Your ability to hear a fire truck, a doorbell, a telephone ringing or your mom coming home is thanks to the teamwork between your ears and your auditory brain.

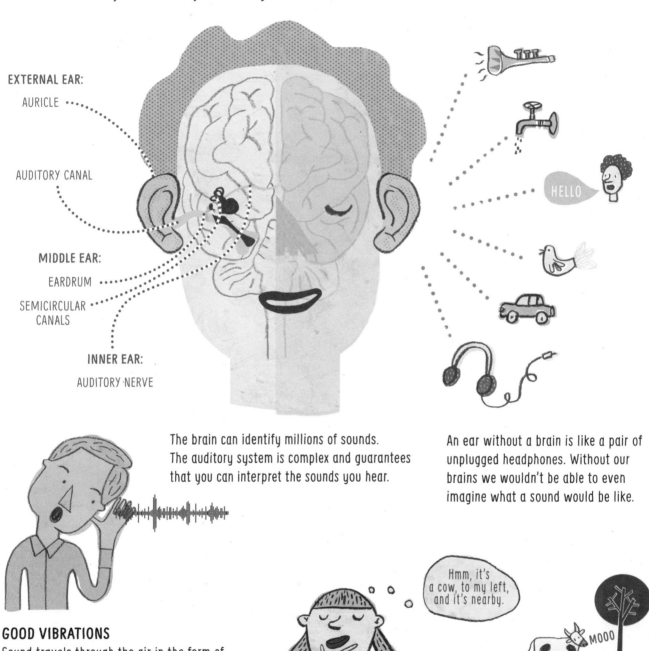

EXTERNAL EAR:
AURICLE

AUDITORY CANAL

MIDDLE EAR:
EARDRUM

SEMICIRCULAR CANALS

INNER EAR:
AUDITORY NERVE

HELLO

The brain can identify millions of sounds. The auditory system is complex and guarantees that you can interpret the sounds you hear.

An ear without a brain is like a pair of unplugged headphones. Without our brains we wouldn't be able to even imagine what a sound would be like.

GOOD VIBRATIONS
Sound travels through the air in the form of waves. When they hit your ears, they are transformed into electrical signals that are sent to the brain. That's where specialized neurons (located in the temporal lobe) "translate" the message. This leads to the perception of the sound: "I can hear!"

Hmm, it's a cow, to my left, and it's nearby.

MOOO

TRANSLATOR
Thanks to our ability to hear, we can notice and identify sounds, their intensity, kind and location. The brain translates the "messages" that the ears send.

CAN I CHOOSE WHAT I HEAR?

The next time you are someplace noisy (a party, a classroom full of rambunctious kids, a concert, etc.), see if you're able to follow your friends' conversation or what your teacher is saying, despite the noise all around you. Think about "turning off" the other sounds while you listen to what you really want to hear.

AUDITORY ILLUSIONS?

The brain receives the information sent by the ears and processes it. It doesn't like to have doubts—it wants to "recognize and understand." Sometimes there is nothing to recognize, so the brain improvises and fills in those empty spaces. This is a kind of auditory illusion. For example, when someone listens to a constant and monotonous sound in a recording, and they think those sounds contain some kind of message, they may end up hearing a message even if there isn't one.

WHY DO WE HAVE TWO EARS?

Most people find it much easier to evaluate distances using both ears instead of just one. Our brains use the difference in the time it takes a sound to reach each ear and the difference in intensity of sound in each ear to determine the location of the sound.

ACTIVITY 1

Ask a friend to cover their eyes and put an earplug in only one ear. Then place a stopwatch or wristwatch at different distances from them and at different angles. Ask them to tell you when they hear the ticking of the watch. Write down the angles and distances.

Then repeat the activity without the earplug. Repeat the experiment with other people. You'll notice differences in auditory sharpness using one or two ears and between different people. It's like your eyes—two are better than one!

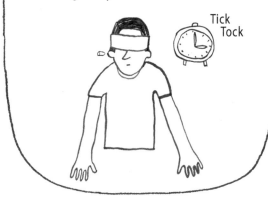

ACTIVITY 2

Fill sets of containers with different contents—two with sand, two with rice, two with coins, two with buttons, etc. Give one container each to a group of friends and have them spread out in the room. Then have one person stand blindfolded in the center of the room while the rest of the people shake their containers one by one. The person in the center has to figure out who has the container that sounds the same as the one they have. Thanks to our sense of hearing, we can recognize different sounds.

TOUCH

My bunny's skin is so soft, and my father's beard is so rough. I like to run my hand over both of them and compare the sensations. My father laughs and says I'm going to be just like him. He gives me a tight hug. I like my mom's hugs and kisses, which are gentle and smooth.

The sense of touch, unlike the other senses, is not located in a single place (like vision in the eyes and hearing in the ears) but instead exists all over your body. Your skin is in direct contact with everything you touch. Through this contact you know if something is hot or cold, smooth or rough, or dry or wet.

MILLIONS OF NERVE ENDINGS

The sense of touch originates in the dermis, which is the layer of skin underneath the epidermis. The dermis has millions of tiny nerve endings that capture information about the objects, textures and temperatures that are in contact with your body. Each of these nerve endings, or receptors, is responsible for sending a particular kind of stimulus to your brain.

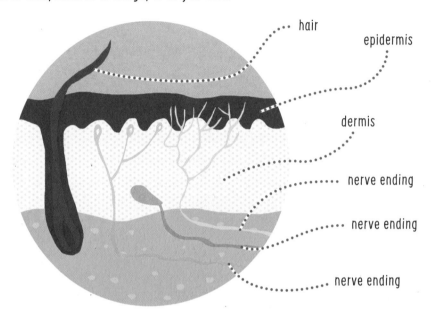

hair
epidermis
dermis
nerve ending
nerve ending
nerve ending

RECEPTORS

There are different receptors for different kinds of sensations. The four primary ones are:

PAIN

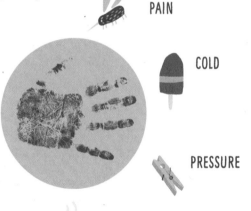

COLD

PRESSURE

HEAT

ELECTRICITY IN YOUR BRAIN

Information from these receptors reaches your brain through electrical impulses that move through the spinal cord. This is how you know if something is smooth, rough, hot, cold or sticky.

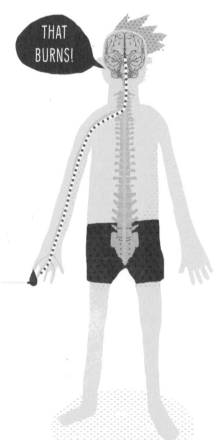

THAT BURNS!

MORE SENSITIVE

Did you know that the sense of touch is different in different parts of the body? Certain areas, like the fingers, lips and face, have more nerve endings than others, making them more sensitive.

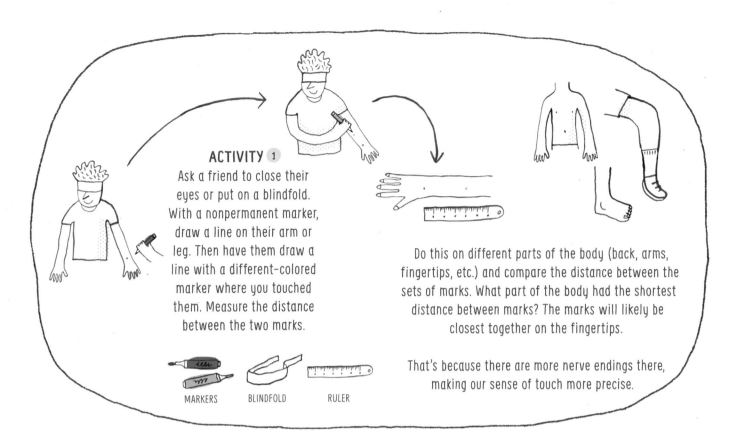

ACTIVITY 1

Ask a friend to close their eyes or put on a blindfold. With a nonpermanent marker, draw a line on their arm or leg. Then have them draw a line with a different-colored marker where you touched them. Measure the distance between the two marks.

Do this on different parts of the body (back, arms, fingertips, etc.) and compare the distance between the sets of marks. What part of the body had the shortest distance between marks? The marks will likely be closest together on the fingertips.

That's because there are more nerve endings there, making our sense of touch more precise.

MARKERS   BLINDFOLD   RULER

ACTIVITY 2

Ask someone to close their eyes or put on a blindfold. Tell them you are about to touch them with different objects and ask them to describe what they feel with each thing. Use something smooth, like an apple, something rough, like a rock, something cold and wet, like an ice cube, and something warm, like a hot water bottle. This will show how there are different receptors on the skin.

APPLE

SEEDS

ICE

HOT WATER BOTTLE

FEATHER

ACTIVITY 3

1   2   3

Fill three bowls with water. Fill the first with cold water and ice, the second with lukewarm water and the third with hot water, like when you're going to have a bath.

Place one hand in the bowl of ice water and the other in the bowl of hot water, and leave them there for two minutes. Then place both hands in the lukewarm water. How do you feel? Do both hands feel the same?

2 MIN

Notice how, despite the temperature being the same, we don't perceive it that way. This happens because the cold receptors on the hand that was in the ice water are "occupied" or busy, so when that hand is placed in the warm water, the heat receptors (which are "unoccupied") start to work, and this makes the water feel hotter to that hand than it does to the other hand.

YOUR BRAIN IS EXCITING!
EMOTIONS

Imagine you're walking down the street and you see a dog rushing toward you and barking. You get scared, and your body undergoes a series of changes that help you confront this emergency. Your heart beats faster, your digestive functions slow down (it wouldn't be a good moment to feel like you need to go to the bathroom, right?), your breathing becomes faster and the level of glucose (a kind of sugar that gives energy) in your blood increases so you can run.

CLEVER EMOTIONS
All these reactions let you act quickly and escape from the dog. They happen because you felt an emotion—fear. Emotions have two components: the physiological response (which generates bodily changes) and the behavioral response (how the emotion makes you act).

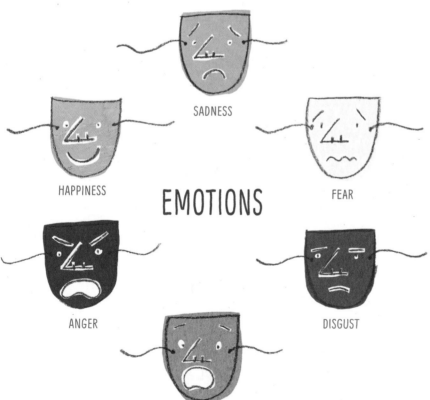

SADNESS

HAPPINESS

EMOTIONS

FEAR

SIX BASIC EMOTIONS
There are six basic emotions, happiness, sadness, fear, anger, surprise and disgust. They are universal, which means they can be found in all cultures, all over the world. Emotions happen automatically, and they're associated with bodily reactions.

ANGER

DISGUST

SURPRISE

TAKE CONTROL

The intensity of an emotion depends as much on the situation as the person. It might be slight, moderate, strong or very intense.

Emotions are not good or bad, but there are good and bad ways of expressing emotions. If you get mad at your sibling because they took your candy, and you hit them on the head with a shoe, that's not the same as talking to them and explaining the importance of their respecting you and your things, but in both situations you're expressing your anger.

Don't let your emotions control you. Instead, take control of your emotions.

EMOTIONAL BEINGS

Emotions come and go. Most of us feel many different emotions over the course of the day. Some might last for seconds. Other emotions might last longer.

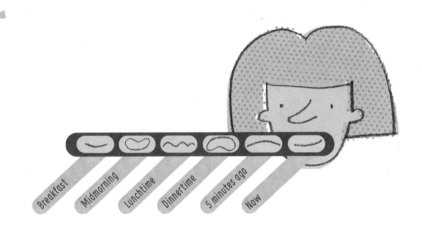

YOUR BRAIN WANTS YOU TO BE HAPPY

The brain creates endorphins, which are a chemical substance that produces pleasure and a feeling of well-being. The amount of endorphins you produce goes up when you exercise, when you laugh, when you're hugged by someone and when you're relaxed, doing such things as meditating, practicing yoga or being out in nature.

DID YOU KNOW THAT LAUGHING IS GOOD FOR YOUR HEALTH?

Laughter originates in the brain. When you laugh, it releases chemical substances that are good for your body. They can make you feel pleasure and feel relaxed. Laughter activates muscles that help your physical well-being—it pushes away stress and makes the people around you feel happy and content. Never forget to do things that make you smile, have a good time and laugh. It is important for your health!

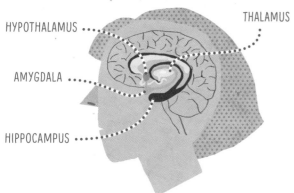

HYPOTHALAMUS

THALAMUS

AMYGDALA

HIPPOCAMPUS

EMOTIONAL BRAIN

The limbic system is the most important area of the brain when it comes to emotions. It has four main parts—the hypothalamus, the amygdala, the thalamus and the hippocampus. These parts are also related to the rest of the brain. The limbic system is the oldest part of the brain, in terms of evolution, and it's here that it gets decided if what we live, learn and memorize is pleasant or unpleasant.

ACTIVITY ①

Look carefully at these faces. Can you see one that shows sadness? Another happiness? Anger? These differences you see are due to the cerebral amygdalas.

SUPER-SCARED

If our amygdalas are too active, we have excessive fears, more than what situations call for.

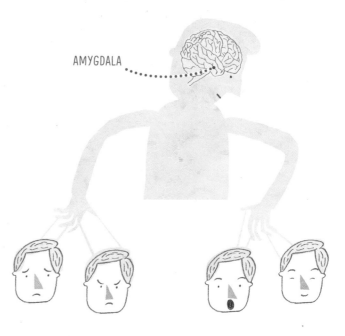

AMYGDALA

THE CEREBRAL AMYGDALAS

They store our deepest emotions, like fear and anguish. They also help us regulate them.

DID YOU KNOW THAT...

...people who have panic attacks or anxiety have amygdalas that are working overtime?
...people who have damaged their amygadalas don't feel fear or consider the risks of their behaviors?

HOW CAN YOU BE MORE AWARE OF YOUR EMOTIONS?

Just as with any other thing in life, emotional awareness improves with practice. Start with these three simple steps.

1. Pay attention to what you're feeling in different situations during the day—happy after making plans with a friend, nervous before an exam, relaxed when you listen to music. Observe each emotion and give it a name in your mind. It only takes a few seconds, and it's a very good practice.

2. Recognize the intensity. After you've recognized, observed and given a name to an emotion, go a step further and figure out how strongly you feel the emotion. You can use a scale of 1 to 10 for this, with 1 being the least and 10 the most intense.

3. Share what you feel with the people who are closest to you. The best way to practice emotional awareness is to put it into words, an ability that will help us to feel closer to our friends, partners, parents, coaches—anyone who is important to you. You can share something very personal or something that is just an everyday emotion.

MUSCULAR FACE

Various facial muscles take part in a smile. They send signals to the brain saying that "the situation is good" and this in turn helps improve your mood.

FEEL TO SURVIVE

Emotions are important for our survival. Fear, for example, produces a fight-or-flight response when you face a dangerous situation. Emotions are important for reproduction (attraction, love) and for raising children (attachment to the baby). They also help us make decisions when faced with complex problems, either avoiding or confronting them.

EMPATHY

Have you ever wondered why you feel pain when you see someone who is hurt? Or why you yawn when you see someone yawn? Or why your mouth starts to water when you see another person eating food you like? Empathy is the ability we have to put ourselves in the place of someone else and to know or understand what they're feeling or even what they might be thinking.

CAN WE READ THE MINDS OF OTHERS?

People with a greater capacity for empathy are those who know how to "read" other people. There are two processes. First we identify someone else's situation. Then we put ourselves in their shoes. Empathy connects us to one another and breaks down barriers between people.

DURING OUR LIFETIMES, WE LEARN ABOUT OUR EMOTIONS AND DEVELOP EMPATHY.

We feel emotions from the moment we're born. Babies and young children react to their emotions with facial expressions or actions like laughing, hugging, crying or kicking. They feel and show emotion, but they don't yet have the ability to give a name to or explain why they feel what they feel.

I am really very upset. I never thought you'd forget my birthday. I never forget yours, and besides...blah, blah, blah...

As we grow older, we become more skilled at understanding our emotions. Instead of reacting without thinking, we can put our feelings into words. With time and practice, we get better at figuring out what we feel and why. This ability is called *emotional awareness*.

In adolescence and adulthood, emotions help us build better relationships. If we are aware of our emotions, we can speak clearly about them and avoid or better resolve conflicts and difficult situations.

EMOTIONAL MIRROR

In our brains there are nerve cells called *mirror neurons*. These motor neurons are activated when we perform an action or see another person performing an action. They can make us feel what that person is feeling. That's why when you see someone get hit, you also "feel" the blow.

MIRROR NEURONS TAKE PART IN:

EMPATHY

HELPING OTHERS

LEARNING BY
IMITATION

THERE'S NO EXCUSE

We all have mirror neurons, and that means we can all use them to improve our empathy and our relationships with others.

Mirror neurons are located in a sector of the frontal lobe and in the parietal lobe, near the area of language. This shows us that human beings are social creatures, because of the very structure and function of the brain.

DO YOU KNOW HOW THESE NEURONS WERE DISCOVERED?

Researchers were recording the activity of motor neurons (that is, those that are activated when we make a movement) in a monkey—activity like, for example, the monkey reaching out to grab a banana. When a researcher walking by grabbed a banana, the neurons in the monkey activated in the same way they had when the monkey himself performed that same action. It was incredible, because the monkey wasn't moving at all! The researchers thought it must be an error, but when they repeated the scene, the monkey did the same thing.

YOUR BRAIN CAN BE SHAPED

The brain is not a machine but rather a muscle that can be trained. When you do the same things a number of times, the connections between the neurons necessary to do these routine actions (such as washing your hair, riding a bicycle or writing in a notebook) become very defined, as if there were a map marked with the streets (or neural pathways) to reach those actions. But what's also incredible is that the brain has the ability to create new pathways every time we practice new habits or challenges. On the other hand, the pathways become weakened when they're not used. This is called *brain plasticity*.

Every time we think, feel or do something, we strengthen a pathway. Habits are neural pathways that are used a lot and therefore make those tasks easy to do.

Our thoughts and abilities create new pathways. Practice and repetition of what we're learning reinforce them. This applies, for example, when you want to learn a new language and you practice speaking it, or when you decide to take guitar lessons or learn how to juggle.

The pathways for things we stop doing become weaker—for example, if you stop playing piano after playing regularly.

MENTAL STIMULATION
It is very important to be mentally stimulated and to face new challenges, or your brain might weaken! Did you know that the risk of dementia decreases if you're stimulating your brain all the time?

SHAPE YOUR BRAIN
Your brain is "plastic," or "moldable." If you don't learn new skills, your brain can't develop neuroplasticity. If you want to keep your brain in top condition, you must give yourself new challenges and activities.

IT'S NEVER TOO LATE FOR NEW THINGS
Neuroplasticity is the brain's ability to change at any age, to be able to reorganize new connections over the course of your entire life.

Vary the way you do your everyday tasks—take a different route to walk to school, go to a different store to buy things, brush your teeth with the opposite hand, sit in a different place in the classroom, etc.

THE SAME OLD THING

NEW PATHS

DON'T FALL INTO ROUTINES

Learn a new language.

Go to museums and exhibits.

Sing. Dance.

Learn to play musical instruments (even if you feel you have no talent for it).

Draw and paint.

4X7-5 +17

Do addition in your head instead of using a calculator.

Read newspapers, books, magazines, stories.

Do puzzles and use logic. Play board games and spend less time on video games.

Learn to juggle, to cook, to garden.

Take walks and discover new places.

Exercise regularly.

YOUR MEMORY

Can you remember your last birthday? Or what your best friend's old house was like? Or the first time you rode a bicycle without training wheels?

Your memory is you. It shapes your identity as a unique being in the world, because everything you've experienced since you were in your mother's womb (whether events, emotions, words, people, places, smells, tastes, stories or dreams) makes up your memory. And it shapes who you are.

HOW IS INFORMATION STORED?
The brain doesn't store information as if it were some piece of furniture with drawers that fill up until there's no more room. What you learn becomes "joined" with other things you already know about the subject, as if you were building a tower with Lego. Your brain stores data, sounds, smells, sensations of touch, images and even feelings. Memories are linked, so that when you remember something you felt, it awakens memories of what you registered with your other senses at that time.

HOW DO WE BRING MEMORIES TO MIND?
A memory is something like a photograph torn into little pieces, each one belonging to the sense or senses involved in its creation. When we recall a memory, we reconstruct the photograph with those pieces, which the brain searches for in the different drawers, or cortexes (auditory, visual, sensory, etc.), in which they are stored.

IT'S NOT PERFECT
Memory is not a perfect copy of what happened. It can be constructed and reconstructed many times.

YOU NEED TO FORGET
Forgetting is normal, even necessary, because it prevents us from accumulating too much useless data. Imagine for a moment what it would be like if you remembered absolutely everything you'd learned and experienced so far in your life. It would be overwhelming! Your brain helps you remember only what is important.

KINDS OF MEMORY

There are many kinds of memory.
The best known are:

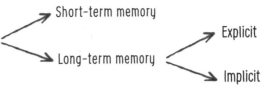

SHORT-TERM

This kind of memory doesn't last long. We
might use it when someone tells us something
that's not very important or doesn't have a
lot of meaning for us. Or it's information we're
going to use right away. You can memorize a
telephone number as you dial it to make a call,
for example, and a short while later you won't
remember it anymore.

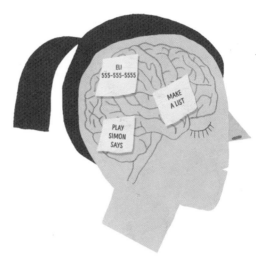

EXPLICIT LONG-TERM MEMORY

Explicit long-term memory is what lets
you tell someone, for example, what film
you saw yesterday, your parents' names, etc.
It's information you can consciously recall
and explain.

IMPLICIT LONG-TERM MEMORY

Implicit long-term memory is something your brain has
learned that you're not consciously aware of. When you
learned to ride a bicycle, for example, you memorized how
to do it, but it would be difficult for you to explain the
steps you took.

EXPLICIT LONG-TERM MEMORY

IMPLICIT LONG-TERM MEMORY

MEMORY PROBLEMS

These two kinds of memory are stored in different places in the brain, so someone might be able to form a short-term
memory but not be able to commit it to long-term memory. People who have suffered brain damage in the areas where
short-term memory is stored can't remember what they discussed 20 minutes ago or the person they were speaking with.

PUT YOUR IMPLICIT MEMORY TO WORK

ACTIVITY 1

Take a pencil and a sheet of paper and write your name and surname with your left hand if you're right-handed and with your right hand if you're a lefty. Do this 10 times in a row, and you'll see that you do it more easily each time. The brain is learning and remembering how to do it.

ACTIVITY 2

Draw a large star on a piece of paper. Then draw an outline of another star inside the existing star, without touching its edges. Repeat this at least five times, and don't rush through each repetition. While you do this, you are likely using your implicit long-term memory, and later you will be able to make the star more easily.

MEMORABLE SENSES

You can improve your memory by using more than one of your senses (sight, hearing, smell, touch, taste) to memorize something. Relate the information to colors, textures, smells and tastes. If you are an oral learner, recite what you want to learn out loud. If you can recite it with a bit of rhythm, so much the better. If you manage to make rhymes, it will be even easier for you to recall.

PUT YOUR SHORT-TERM MEMORY TO WORK

ACTIVITY 1

Look at these series of numbers for one minute and try to memorize them, starting with level 1. What level did you get to? Generally a person can only remember four to six numbers for a short time, but this depends on their age and other factors.

LEVEL 1	0-9-3
LEVEL 2	8-5-4-7-9
LEVEL 3	1-5-2-9-5-4-3

ACTIVITY ②

Look at this illustration for three minutes and then, after covering it, try to remember as many objects as you can. How many could you remember?

Now try and remember them again, but do it by grouping the objects by kind—for example, household objects, living things, articles worn on the body, etc. Now how many could you remember?

You probably did better the second time. That's because your brain can retain more information if it makes associations between the elements you want to remember.

ACTIVITY ③

Read the words in list 1. Then cover them and write down as many as you can remember. Do the same with lists 2 and 3.

LIST 1	LIST 2	LIST 3
CROCODILE	ANGER	CAMO
APPLE	BELIEF	LEPEA
ARROW	BOREDOM	MOSES
BABY	POSSIBILITY	VONTAN
BIRD	CONCEPT	CILOPAS
BOOK	EFFORT	REDONE
BUTTERFLY	FATE	POLAS
CAR	FREEDOM	TILESA
CORN	GLORY	UBESO
FLOWER	HAPPINESS	INAMI
HAMMER	HONOR	BOLER
HOUSE	HOPE	PLONA
COIN	IDEA	BRAFE
MICROSCOPE	INTEREST	CRORE
OCEAN	KNOWLEDGE	BLEDUN
PENCIL	MOOD	EVOLI
SHOES	MORAL	SOSDE
TABLE	THEORIES	BIDARE
WINDOW	TRUTH	NIUMIE
ROCK	MERCY	NASOL

What did you notice? Did you remember more words from list 1, list 2 or list 3?

It is easier to remember words that are more specific because you can imagine them in your mind. This is harder to do with the abstract words and even more difficult with the nonsense words.

IMPROVING YOUR MEMORY

We remember what's important or has significance for us. It's easier to remember something if you know why it's necessary to learn it. Perhaps you'll be tested on it, or it will be useful to you, or the subject interests you.

For example, if you need to remember a recipe, you might read the recipe aloud, explain the steps to someone else and make the meal a few times. It's about making this knowledge your own, not just repeating it but understanding and living it, enjoying what you're learning. It's pleasant to do things with enthusiasm and have fun while you do it!

TRICKS TO STRENGTHEN YOUR MEMORY
Associate an image with what you want to memorize (the more absurd or fun it is, the more you'll remember it). For example, if you go to a shopping center and your parents park on level E, space 4, and you want to remember where your car is parked, use an image of four elephants on top of your car!

THE TRAIN OR CHAIN
This technique helps you remember a series of words. You think in images and then link them. For example, if you have to buy various things at the grocery store—milk, eggs, cheese and oranges—you might imagine an orange tree with lots of oranges and a chicken sitting on a nest of eggs. Then, for your milk and cheese, you might picture a cow beside the tree and a farmer who will milk her.

STEP BY STEP

It's easier to remember information if it's divided into small parts. For example, if you have to remember a number, you might divide it up and associate the smaller numbers with some specific situations. If the number is 213658174, you might divide it into 21, the day your little brother was born; 365, the number of days in a year; 81, your grandfather's age; 7, the number of days in a week; and 4, the number of cousins you have.

BUILD A TOWER

When you want to learn something that's difficult, it is much easier if you start with the easy parts. Practice explaining it to your friends and family. As if it were a Lego tower, start with the base—the most basic. Then follow with the middle sections, which are where the information (or the tower) starts to get more complicated. By the time you reach the final, most difficult part, you're ready to understand the most complex ideas.

TAKE FRACTIONS, FOR EXAMPLE

First you need to understand the idea of something being whole, like an apple. Then see what happens when you divide it in two, which gives you halves. And what happens when you divide those halves again, and so on. This will help you learn to add fractions.

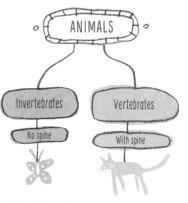

BE CREATIVE

When you study, you'll remember information better if it's presented in an attractive way, with colors, different kinds of letters, in sections, etc.

MNEMONIC SENTENCES

Make a sentence with the first letter of every word in a series. For example, if you need to learn the planets of the solar system in order, starting with the ones closest to the sun, you could invent the following sentence:

MOTHER VISITS EVERY MONDAY, JUST STAYS UNTIL NOON.

MOTHER	MERCURY
VISITS	VENUS
EVERY →	EARTH
MONDAY	MARS
JUST	JUPITER
STAYS	SATURN
UNTIL	URANUS
NOON	NEPTUNE

EACH THING IN ITS PLACE

You can help yourself remember things if you start by remembering where you were when something happened, what the place looked like, what you were doing, etc. This is called *context-dependent memory*. For example, studies show that if students learn something while underwater, they can remember it better later if they're underwater instead of on dry land. Isn't that incredible? If you want to remember where you left your pencil, retrace your steps and think about where you were during the day and what you were doing.

CONDUCTOR OF THE ORCHESTRA
EXECUTIVE FUNCTIONS

Can you imagine an orchestra of musicians without a conductor? It would be pretty chaotic, because the conductor organizes the orchestra. Some instruments start before others while the rest keep silent. Then one hears a second set of instruments, and the first stops. In short, the orchestra is harmonic because there is someone who keeps track of the big picture. Just as an orchestra conductor organizes and controls the musicians' performance, or an air-traffic controller regulates the flights entering and leaving an airport, executive functions are mental skills that control and coordinate our behavior. They are located primarily in the frontal lobes but are connected to other regions of the brain.

THE EXECUTIVE FUNCTIONS INCLUDE:

1. REASONING
We are constantly receiving information—noises, smells, sounds, etc. This function is what allows us to analyze these different pieces of information and recognize the possible connections between them.

2. PLANNING
This executive function is what lets us think ahead and come up with a plan of action to get what we want.

3. GOAL-SETTING
Thanks to this skill, we are able to decide where to direct our behavior.

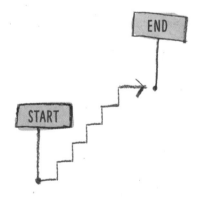

4. DECISION-MAKING
We are always receiving information, and therefore we have many choices for what to do, how to act, where to go, etc. This executive function is what lets us determine what option to choose from all the ones we have.

5. TASK INITIATION AND COMPLETION
This executive function lets us start and finish an activity, controlling the distractions or difficulties we encounter.

6. ORGANIZATION
All the information we receive, from the time we wake up until we go to sleep, is ordered efficiently and usefully thanks to this executive function.

7. SELF-MONITORING

Gymnasts spin on the beam and keep their balance by maintaining focus so they don't fall. They can do this thanks to self-monitoring. This ability lets you keep your attention on what you're doing and observe how you're doing it.

8. INHIBITION (IMPULSE CONTROL)

Inhibition is the executive function that allows us to resist certain impulses, like when someone bothers you and you want to give them a push. Thanks to inhibition, you can control yourself and keep from doing certain things.

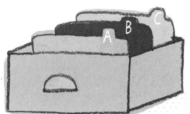
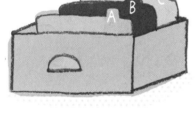

9. WORKING MEMORY

This is the ability to store information on both a verbal and nonverbal level. Verbal memory is the reason you can remember your friend's phone number. Nonverbal memory allows you to remember that you were going to start your math homework as you answer a text from that friend while walking to your room.

10. ANTICIPATION

This ability lets us think about the results of an action and/or its consequences before doing it. For example, if you get angry and feel like yelling at your mother, you can think before doing it and realize that yelling won't solve anything.

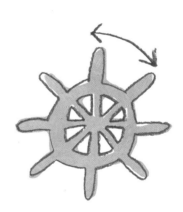

11. FLEXIBILITY

The ability to be flexible is what lets you change your way of thinking or acting when faced with unexpected situations or changes.

THOMAS USES HIS EXECUTIVE FUNCTIONS

Thomas has to turn in his homework tomorrow for language arts class. He has to make a vocabulary list of 10 words from the story, answer 5 questions about the story and write a different ending for it.

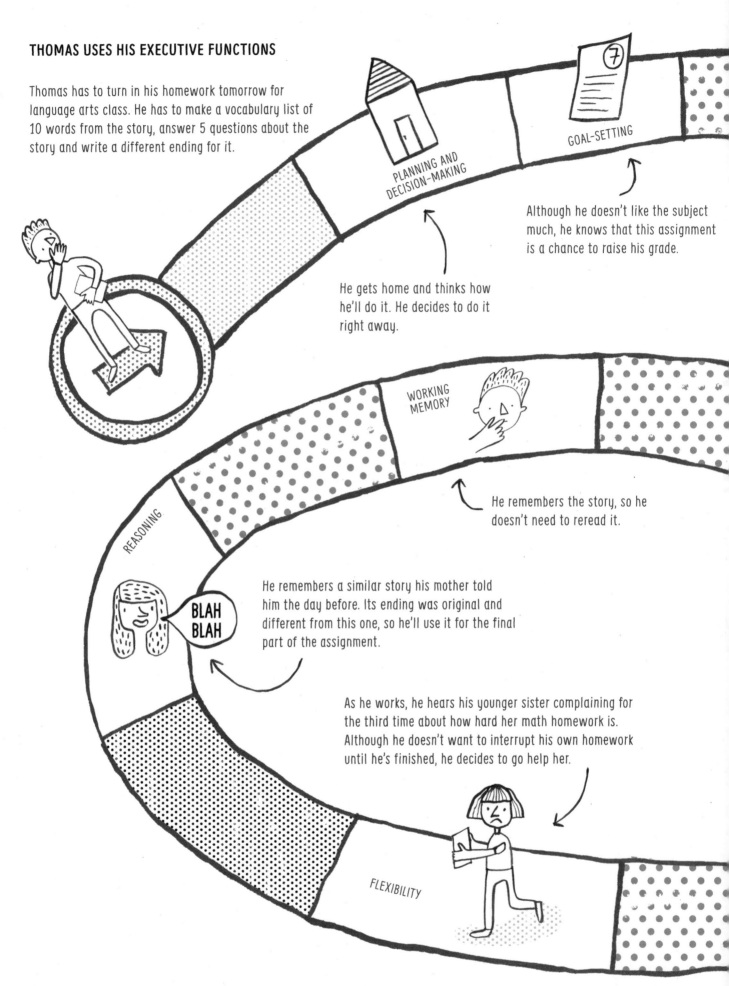

Although he doesn't like the subject much, he knows that this assignment is a chance to raise his grade.

He gets home and thinks how he'll do it. He decides to do it right away.

He remembers the story, so he doesn't need to reread it.

He remembers a similar story his mother told him the day before. Its ending was original and different from this one, so he'll use it for the final part of the assignment.

As he works, he hears his younger sister complaining for the third time about how hard her math homework is. Although he doesn't want to interrupt his own homework until he's finished, he decides to go help her.

TASK INITIATION

He goes to his desk and sets out what he needs to do his homework.

ANTICIPATION AND INHIBITION

He turns off his cell phone because he knows he will be distracted by messages and wants to finish his homework before mealtime.

ORGANIZATION

He decides to start with the vocabulary because he knows it will be the easiest part, then he'll answer the questions, and finally he'll write the new ending.

After working for 40 minutes, he looks over how much he has left to do. If he keeps working at this rate, he'll be done in 30 or 40 minutes.

SELF-MONITORING

PLANNING

When he gets back to his desk, he decides to concentrate fully, because he wants to have an hour of free time when he's done with his homework.

GOAL-SETTING

TASK FINISHED!
Now he's free for the rest of the afternoon!

Card and board games (chess, checkers, dominoes, etc).

Games and physical activities (hide-and-seek, tag). Organized sports (like soccer, volleyball and basketball), yoga, jump rope, martial arts (like tae kwon do, etc).

Dance routines, coordination and rhythm games (for example, clapping to different rhythms).

Imitation games, singing in rounds.

Playing a musical instrument, singing in a choir.

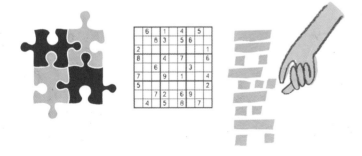

Silent activities that require strategy—puzzles, riddles, sudoku, crossword puzzles.

SLEEP (ALSO GOOD FOR YOUR MOOD)

Have you noticed there are days when you're more distracted or in a bad mood? If you try to remember one of those days carefully, you might realize you slept poorly the night before. Pay attention to the ways you change depending on how many hours of sleep you get at night.

HOW TO TAKE CARE OF YOUR BRAIN

The brain, like the rest of the body, needs you to take care of it. Just as you need to eat your vegetables and exercise to stay healthy, there are also things you can (and should!) do to take care of your brain.

EXERCISE
Aerobic physical exercise (running, riding a bicycle, jumping, hurdling, etc.) is one of the best ways to keep your brain young and active—the brain gets more oxygen when you exercise. It should be regular—at least 45 minutes three times a week for adults, and one hour per day for children. Remember that playing tag, ball, etc. are physical activities that take care of your brain! These activities also increase your ability to focus your attention, your memory and your ability to learn. (Tell that to your parents and grandparents! It's never too late to start!)

EAT HEALTHILY
Choose healthy foods (fruits, vegetables, legumes, low-fat milk, fish, nuts). Avoid junk food, and don't skip meals. Drink between six and eight glasses of water every day. The brain needs food and water to work better.

SLEEP
Sleep 10 to 11 hours every day. It's very important to sleep at night. Avoid going to bed late and then waking up late—going to sleep at two in the morning and waking up at noon is not the same as going to bed at nine and waking up at seven. In both cases you sleep for 10 hours, but it's much better for the brain to be awake during the day and to sleep at night.

TAKE CARE OF IT
When you're a teen, avoid drinking alcohol, smoking cigarettes or marijuana and using other drugs. These affect your brain at a time when it's still developing and they interfere with its development processes.

PROTECT IT
When you ride a bike or go rollerblading, ice skating or skiing, never forget to wear a helmet to protect your brain from the impact of falls. Always wear your seat belt in cars and on buses.

TALK TO OTHERS
If you feel sad, afraid or lonely, or have difficulties sleeping, talk to your parents. And if that's not enough, ask them to take you to see a specialist. These problems also affect your brain.

INDEX

activities and games
  about our senses, 12, 16, 22, 24, 26, 28, 32
  improving memory, 43—46
  and learning, 39—40, 43, 51
  listening skills, 14, 30
  and movement, 10, 18, 20
  and self-control, 10
adult brains, 6, 37
amygdala, 13, 35
anticipation of consequences, 8, 9, 10, 48
attention and focus, 9, 20, 48
auditory illusions, 30
auditory system, 29

back brain, 7
behaviors
  changing habits, 39—40
  and emotions, 33—36
  impulse control, 9, 10, 48
body functions, 19—20
body odor, 28
body temperature, 19
brain. See human brain
brain cells, 5—6
brain complexity, 5—6
brain damage
  to amygdala, 13, 35
  and information transfer, 20
  lack of oxygen, 2
  loss of sense of touch, 12
  and memory, 14, 42
  and muscle control, 18
  and personality, 10, 14
  prevention, 4, 52
  and speech, 14
  and vision, 16
brain development, 6, 52
brain plasticity, 39—40

brain stem, 8, 19—20
brain structure, 7—8
breathing, 19—20

central nervous system, 4, 7—8
cerebellum, 8, 17—18
cerebral lobes, 8
children and youth
  babies, 6, 37
  brain development, 6
  and emotional awareness, 35, 36, 37
  reaching goals, 49—50
cognitive skills, 47—51
color, 15, 23
communication within the body, 3, 5, 7, 19—20
consequences, anticipation of, 8, 9, 10, 48
coordination and balance, 9, 11, 17—18
creativity, 7

decision-making
  homework example, 49—50
  impulse control, 9, 10, 48

Einstein, Albert, 2
emotions
  awareness of, 35, 36, 37
  of babies, 37
  and bonding, 36
  and the brain, 1, 9, 33—36
  and empathy, 9, 37—38
  getting support, 52
  role of amygdala, 13, 35
empathy, 9, 37—38
endorphins, 34
evolution, 2, 35
executive functions
  about, 47—48
  problem-solving, 49—50
exercise, 34, 52

fear, 33, 35, 36
fight-or-flight response, 36
focus and attention, 9, 20, 48
frontal lobe, 8, 9—10
front brain, 7

Gage, Phineas, 10
glia cells, 5
goals, reaching, 49—50

habits, changing of, 39—40
happiness, 33, 34
health. See also brain damage
  and changing habits, 39—40
  excessive fears, 35
  and exercise, 34, 52
  and laughter, 34
  and smiling, 36
  tips, 52
hearing
  and the brain, 13, 21
  ear structure, 29
  focused, 30
helmets, 4, 52
hippocampus, 2, 13, 35
human brain
  changes to, 6, 39—40
  characteristics, 1—2
  gender differences, 2
  nervous system, 3—6
  structure, 7—8
humans, prehistoric, 2, 25, 36
hypothalamus, 35

impulse control, 9, 10, 48
information transfer
  and the brain stem, 19—20
  and nerves, 3, 5, 7, 31
injuries. See also brain damage
  and information transfer, 20

injuries (*continued*)
    loss of sense of touch, 12
    prevention, 4, 52
involuntary systems, 20

language skills, 1, 9, 13–14
laughter, 34
learning
    and brain activity, 6
    new pathways, 39–40
    tools, 45–46
left hemisphere of brain, 7
limbic system, 35
long-term memory, 9, 13, 42

memorization tools, 45–46
memory
    and the brain, 9, 11, 13–14, 41–42, 48
    improving, 43–46
    role of hippocampus, 2, 13
    and smells, 27
mirror neurons, 38
motor neurons, 19, 20, 38

nerve cells, 38
nerve endings, 31
nervous system
    central, 4, 7–8
    electrical impulses, 3, 21, 31
neurons
    about, 5–6, 39–40
    mirror neurons, 38
    motor neurons, 19, 20, 38
    sensory neurons, 19
    storing of memories, 41
neuroplasticity, 39–40

occipital lobe, 8, 15–16
odors, 21, 27–28
olfactory receptors, 27

optical illusions, 24
oxygen requirement, 2
panic attacks, 35
pain receptors, 12, 31
parietal lobe, 8, 11–12
personality
    changes to, 4, 10
    and memory, 41
physiological responses, 33
planning and organizing, 9, 47
prehistoric humans, 2, 25, 36

rational thought, 2, 7, 39
reading and writing, 12, 13, 15
reasoning, 9, 47
relationships, 9, 36, 37–38
resources, 54
right hemisphere of brain, 7

scents, 21, 27–28
self-awareness
    of emotions, 35, 36, 37
    focus and attention, 9, 48
    and mood, 34, 51
self-control
    and emotions, 34
    homework example, 49–50
    impulse control, 9, 10, 48
sensory neurons, 19
sensory organs
    about, 21–22
    and illusions, 24, 30
    and memory, 41
short-term memory, 42, 43
skin, 31–32
skull, 4, 24
sleep, 51, 52
smell
    and the brain, 21, 27–28
    and taste, 26

smiling, 36
speech, 13, 14
spinal cord, 3, 19
subconscious body functions, 19–20
synapses, 5

taste
    and the brain, 21, 25–26
    and other senses, 26
    and the tongue, 25
temperature receptors, 31, 32
temporal lobe, 8, 13–14
thalamus, 35
thoughts, 2, 7, 39
touch
    and the brain, 11, 12
    loss of sense of, 12
    receptors, 21, 31–32

vision
    and the brain, 15–16, 21
    and color, 15, 23
    eye structure, 23–24
    and taste, 26

working memory, 48

youth
    brain development, 6
    and emotional awareness, 35, 36, 37
    reaching goals, 49–50

RESOURCES

If you want to learn more about the brain, you can check out these web pages:

Brain Facts, KonnectHQ: Fun Brain Facts for Kids
scienceforkidsclub.com/brain.html

DK Find Out!
dkfindout.com

Ducksters: Biology for Kids: The Human Brain
ducksters.com/science/brain.php

Easy Science for Kids: Fun Facts about the Brain for Kids
easyscienceforkids.com/all-about-your-amazing-brain

KidsHealth: Your Brain & Nervous System
kidshealth.org/en/kids/brain.html

National Geographic Kids: Your Amazing Brain!
natgeokids.com/uk/discover/science/general-science/human-brain

Neuroscience For Kids: Divisions of the Nervous System
faculty.washington.edu/chudler/nsdivide.html

Neuroscience For Kids: Types of Neurons (Nerve Cells)
faculty.washington.edu/chudler/cells.html

Originally published in Spanish in 2019 by Editorial Amanuta under the title *Tu cerebro es genial*.

Published in Canada and the United States in 2023 by Orca Book Publishers.
orcabook.com

Library and Archives Canada Cataloguing in Publication
Title: Your brain is amazing : how the human mind works / Esperanza Habinger ;
illustrated by Sole Sebastián ; translated by Lawrence Schimel.
Other titles: Tu cerebro es genial.
English Names: Habinger, Esperanza, author. | Sebastián, Soledad, illustrator. | Schimel, Lawrence, translator.
Description: Translation of: Tu cerebro es genial. | Includes bibliographical references and index.
Identifiers: Canadiana (print) 20220189102 | Canadiana (ebook) 20220189110 |
ISBN 9781459832176 (hardcover) | ISBN 9781459832183 (PDF) | ISBN 9781459832190 (EPUB)
Subjects: LCSH: Brain—Juvenile literature.
Classification: LCC QP376 .H3313 2023 | DDC j612.8/2—dc23

Library of Congress Control Number: 2022934631

Summary: This illustrated nonfiction book for middle-grade readers is a comprehensive overview of the brain. It looks at the science behind how it works, how it directs our day-to-day lives and how much we don't know about this key organ in our bodies.

Orca Book Publishers is committed to reducing the consumption of nonrenewable resources in the production of our books. We make every effort to use materials that support a sustainable future.

Orca Book Publishers gratefully acknowledges the support for its publishing programs provided by the following agencies: the Government of Canada, the Canada Council for the Arts and the Province of British Columbia through the BC Arts Council and the Book Publishing Tax Credit.

The author and publisher have made every effort to ensure that the information in this book was correct at the time of publication. The author and publisher do not assume any liability for any loss, damage or disruption caused by errors or omissions. Every effort has been made to trace copyright holders and to obtain their permission for the use of copyrighted material. The publisher apologizes for any errors or omissions and would be grateful if notified of any corrections that should be incorporated in future reprints or editions of this book.

We acknowledge the financial support of the Government of Canada through the National Translation Program for Book Publishing, an initiative of the Roadmap for Canada Official Languages 2013–2018: Education, Immigration, Communities, for our translation activities.

Cover and interior artwork by Sole Sebastián
Edited by Kirstie Hudson
Translated by Lawrence Schimel

Printed and bound in Canada.

26 25 24 23 • 1 2 3 4

Did you like this book? Do you feel you've learned more about yourself (your brain) and the human body? That's great! That's why we made it!

ESPERANZA HABINGER is a fan of science. She studied medicine and then specialized in child and teen psychiatry. Esperanza has always been interested in sharing this knowledge, and that's why she's taken part in many conferences through the Society of Child and Adolescent Psychiatry. She is currently the vice president of the Chilean Society of Bipolar Disorders, but what she is most passionate about is talking with kids and teenagers about how they feel and what problems they have. This is her first science book for young readers. Esperanza lives in Santiago, Chile.

SOLE SEBASTIÁN studied design, but she always liked to draw, so she decided to become an illustrator. Since then she's devoted herself to illustrating for books and magazines. She likes to explore different techniques because there are many different ways to tell stories. She has also given workshops for both kids and adults. Sole lives in Tulsa, Chile.